中国思想文化术语多语种对外翻译
标准化建设项目成果
CHINESE THINKING AND CULTURE
MULTILINGUAL TERMINOLOGY DATABASE

中华源·河南故事

CHINESE CIVILIZATION
Stories from Henan

少林拳法入门

AN INTRODUCTION TO SHAOLIN QUAN

河南省人民政府外事办公室　编

河南大学出版社
HENAN UNIVERSITY PRESS
·郑州·

图书在版编目（CIP）数据

中华源·河南故事．少林拳法入门：汉英对照 / 河南省人民政府外事办公室编．-- 郑州：河南大学出版社，2023.8

ISBN 978-7-5649-5657-8

Ⅰ．①中… Ⅱ．①河… Ⅲ．①地方文化—河南—通俗读物—汉、英②少林拳—通俗读物—汉、英 Ⅳ．①G127.61-49 ②G852.15-49

中国国家版本馆CIP数据核字（2023）第197567号

少林拳法入门

SHAOLIN QUANFA RUMEN

责任编辑 杨光辉

责任校对 屈琳玉

封面设计 翟淼淼

版式设计 郭 灿

出版发行 河南大学出版社

地址：郑州市郑东新区商务外环中华大厦2401号　　邮编：450046

电话：0371-86059701（营销部）

0371-86059750（高等教育与职业教育分公司）

网址：hupress.henu.edu.cn

排　　版 河南大学出版社设计排版部

印　　刷 河南华彩实业有限公司

版　　次 2023年8月第1版　　**印　　次** 2023年8月第1次印刷

开　　本 710 mm×1010 mm　1/16　　**印　　张** 11.75

字　　数 248千字　　**定　　价** 58.00元

“中华源·河南故事”系列丛书编委会

中华源·河南故事·少林拳法入门

主　　编　刘少鹏

副 主 编　刘少菲　田　冲　张志莹

中文撰稿　田　冲　张志莹　冯俊杰　姚亚行　张献科

英文翻译　梅　冰　杨书霞　杨广俊　方金丹　于雪梅

英文审校　[美]Rex Troumbley

The Editorial Committee
Chinese Civilization
Stories from Henan

Chinese Civilization
Stories from Henan
An Introduction to Shaolin Quan

Editor-in-Chief Liu Shaopeng

Associate Editors-in-Chief Liu Shaofei Tian Chong Zhang Zhiying

Writers Tian Chong Zhang Zhiying Feng Junjie Yao Yaxing Zhang Xianke

Translators Mei Bing Yang Shuxia Yang Guangjun Fang Jindan Yu Xuemei

Translation Proofreader Rex Troumbley(U. S.)

总　序

中国是世界四大文明古国之一，也是世界上唯一的古代文明传统未曾中断的国家。河南省地处中国中东部，是中华文明和中华民族的重要发祥地，在中国五千年的文明史上，河南作为国家政治、经济、文化的中心就长达三千多年。从某种意义上讲，一部河南史就是半部中国史。这里是中华人文始祖黄帝的故乡，是古丝绸之路的东方起点，是少林功夫和陈氏太极的发源地，这里创建了中国历史上最早的都城，镌刻了中国最古老的文字，诞生了中国最初的商业文明。

伴随着新时代的荣光，河南经济社会发展迅速，人民生活水平显著提升，这是河南人民自力更生、艰苦奋斗的历史结果，也是对外开放带来的益处。河南经济社会的发展、人民生活方式的改变都植根于深层次的文化积淀。为了让世界更多地了解河南，让河南更好地走向世界，2018年以来，河南省人民政府外事办公室认真研析了这片古老土地上的历史文化资源和时代风貌，组织各领域权威专家学者，编译了“中华源·河南故事”中外文系列丛书，选取黄河文化、河洛文化、老子、庄子、黄帝、少林功夫、太极拳、中医、汉字、丝绸之路、古都、农业、大运河、文物、陶瓷、青铜器、手工艺、书法、杂技、豫菜、豫剧、脱贫攻坚、空中丝绸之路、航空城、南水北调、中原粮谷、红旗渠、焦裕禄等多个主题，力图以故事的方式向世界展现一个立体、全面、真实的河南。

当今世界，人类文明无论是在物质还是在精神方面都取得了巨大进步，特别是物质的极大丰富，这在古代世界是完全不能想象的。同时，当代人类也面临着许多突出的难题，比如，贫富差距持续扩大，物欲追求奢华无度，个人主义恶性膨胀，社会诚信不断消减，伦理道德每况愈下，人与自然关系日趋紧张，等等。要解决这些难题，不仅需要运用人类今天的智慧和力量，而且需要运用人类历史上积累和储存的智慧和力量。河南历史文化底蕴深厚、包容性强，在今天仍极具现实意义。中原文化蕴含的思想智慧有助于修身养性，推动人类社会进步发展，焦裕禄精神、红旗渠精神所体现的为民爱民、艰苦奋斗的价值取向是构建人类命运共同体的力量源泉。我们期待与读者们一起从河南故事中汲取更多的智慧和力量，共同创造更加美好的未来。

Series Foreword

China is one of the four ancient civilizations in the world, and is also the only country in the world where the ancient civilization has not been interrupted. Located in east-central China, Henan Province is an important cradle for the Chinese nation and Chinese civilization. In the course of the five thousand years of Chinese history, for more than three thousand years it served as the political, economic and cultural center of the country and therefore, as generally accepted, represents half of the history of China. Henan is the native place of Yellow Emperor, the cradle of Chinese culture, the starting point of the ancient Silk Road in the east, and the birthplace of Shaolin Kungfu and Chen-style Taijiquan—typical examples of the world-renowned Chinese martial arts. It was here that the earliest capital city in China was founded, the oldest Chinese characters engraved, and the earliest commerce took shape.

In the new era, Henan has witnessed rapid growth in its economy and remarkable improvement of people's living conditions owing to the national reform and opening-up policy and unremitting endeavors of the people. Modern economic achievements and social development as well as the changes of way of life could be traced back to its traditional values and cultural heritages. To enable people from other countries to understand Henan, and let the Province integrate more efficiently into the world development, the Foreign Affairs Office of the People's Government of Henan Province has organized teams of authoritative experts and scholars in relevant fields to compile this *Chinese Civilization: Stories from Henan* in Chinese and foreign languages since 2018 by crystallizing the excellence of traditions and outstanding features of modern development. The book series include *The Yellow River Culture*, *Heluo Culture*, *Laozi*, *Zhuangzi*, *The Yellow Emperor*, *Shaolin Kungfu*, *Taijiquan*, *Traditional Chinese Medicine*,

Chinese Characters, *The Silk Road*, *Ancient Chinese Capitals*, *Feeding the People—Agriculture*, *The Grand Canal*, *Cultural Heritage*, *Ceramic*, *Bronze*, *Handicraft Art*, *Calligraphy*, *Acrobatics*, *Henan Cuisine*, *Henan Opera*, *Poverty Alleviation*, *Silk Road in the Air*, *Zhengzhou—An Aviation City*, *South-to-North Water Diversion*, *Grain of the Central Plains*, *Man-Made River—Hongqiqu Canal*, *A Model Official—Jiao Yulu*, etc., presenting a panoramic picture of the Province.

In today's world, human civilization has made great progress in both material accumulation and ethical advancement, and the great abundance of materials today, especially, is beyond the imagination of the ancient people. At the same time, however, modern people are also confronted with a lot of problems, such as the widening gap between the rich and the poor, the indulgence in pursuit of luxury and extravagance, the undesirable extension of individualism, the decline of social integrity, and the increasingly tense relationship between man and nature. To solve the problems, we need to draw on the wisdom and powers developed today as well as those accumulated in the past. Henan is endowed with rich historical and cultural heritages characterized by its inclusiveness, and such heritages remain significant today. The intelligence and wisdom in Henan culture are conducive to self-cultivation and to the promotion of social development. The spirit of serving the people and relentless struggle, as embodied in Jiao Yulu and the man-made river—Hongqiqu Canal provides source of strength for building a community with a shared future for mankind. It is our hope that wisdom and strength from Henan stories could lead us to a shared brilliant future.

前　言

常言道："天下功夫出少林，中国功夫甲天下。"少林拳是中国传统拳种之一，少林拳因少林寺而得名，是在中国古代健身技击术的基础上，集百家之长，经长期研练而形成的最有影响力的拳种之一。少林拳指的是少林拳派，其中包含了多种传统武术套路，是融合各种传统技法形成的相对稳定的拳法套路。

少林拳发源于嵩山少林寺，可追溯到北魏时期，距今已有1500多年的历史。少林寺自建成以来，僧众参战和护寺之迹不绝，隋朝末年，少林寺十三武僧助唐王李世民击败王世充后，少林寺逐渐有了名气。到了明朝，少林寺已经以武功名扬天下。明末清初，少林拳广泛吸收北方许多拳派的精华，在本寺武功的基础上加以融合，最终形成了内容博深、技艺精湛的少林拳系。少林拳以其刚健有力、朴实无华和利于技击而在国内外享有盛名。

1982年电影《少林寺》的公映使少林武术热居高不下，国内外慕名前来学习少林武术的习武者络绎不绝，各种武校、武馆应运而生。两年一届的郑州国际少林武术节吸引了来自世界数十个国家和地区、上百个武术团队的上万名运动员参加，成为世界武术的盛会；国家体育总局组织编写的"中国少林拳竞赛套路"丛书使少林拳系列走上了竞赛的平台，《中国武术段位制系列教程·少林拳》则对少林拳的传承与发展、推广与普及起到积极的推动作用。

本书从少林拳的基本概念、术语出发，详细讲解少林拳的基本动作、代表性套路，图文并茂、通俗易懂。本书不仅适合国内武术学校学生使用，而且可作为海外武术爱好者学习少林武术的辅助资料或自学材料。本书与《中华源·河南故事·少林功夫》相辅相成，分别从文化和技术层面展现少林武术的魅力，可参照阅读。

Preface

As the saying goes, "All martial arts in China originated from Shaolin, and Chinese martial arts are supreme in the world." Named after the Shaolin Temple, Shaolin quan is one of China' traditional boxing styles. It represents one of the most influential boxing styles developed on the foundation of ancient Chinese fitness and combat techniques, incorporating the strengths of various schools through long-term practice. Shaolin quan also stands for the Shaolin school, which includes a wide range of traditional martial arts routines. It is a relatively stable system of boxing techniques formed by the integration of various traditional methods.

Shaolin quan originated from the Shaolin Temple located near Mount Song, with a history that can be traced back to the Northern Wei Dynasty, over 1500 years ago. Since its establishment, the monastery's monks have been involved in combat and the protection of the temple. By the end of the Sui Dynasty, after thirteen warrior monks from the temple helped Li Shimin, who later became the second emperor of the Tang Dynasty, defeat Wang Shichong, the monastery gradually gained fame. By the Ming Dynasty, it had become renowned throughout China for its martial arts. From the late Ming to the early Qing Dynasty, Shaolin quan widely absorbed the essence of many northern boxing styles. It integrated these with the monastery's martial arts practices to form a profound and skilled system of Shaolin quan. Known for its vigorous, straightforward, and combat-effective techniques, Shaolin quan nowadays enjoys a prestigious reputation both domestically and internationally.

The release of the movie *The Shaolin Temple* in 1982 sparked a continued interest in Shaolin martial arts. Enthusiasts from both China and abroad flocked to learn Shaolin martial arts, leading to the emergence of various martial arts schools and academies. The biennial Zhengzhou International Shaolin Kungfu Festival, attracting tens of thousands of participants from dozens of countries and regions and hundreds of martial arts teams, has become a grand event in the world of martial arts. *Series of Chinese Shaolin Quan Competition Routines*, compiled by the General Administration of Sport of China, places Shaolin quan on a competitive platform. Further, *Textbook Series of Chinese Wushu Duanwei System: Shaolin Quan* plays a significant role in the inheritance, development, and popularity of Shaolin quan.

This book begins with the basic concepts and terms of Shaolin quan, providing a detailed explanation of its fundamental movements and representative routines, accompanied by illustrations and written in accessible language. It is not only suitable for students at domestic martial arts schools but also serves as supplementary material or a self-study guide for overseas martial arts enthusiasts interested in learning Shaolin martial arts. The book complements *The Source of Chinese Civilization: Stories from Henan—Shaolin Kungfu,* showcasing the allure of Shaolin martial arts from both cultural and technical perspectives.

目　录　　Contents

第一章　少林拳概述　001

一、少林寺与少林拳　002

二、少林拳的历史渊源　002

三、少林拳的技法要领　008

四、学拳旨要　014

Chapter 1　Overview of Shaolin Quan　001

Ⅰ.The Shaolin Temple and Shaolin Quan　003

Ⅱ.Historical Origins of Shaolin Quan　005

Ⅲ.Key Techniques of Shaolin Quan　009

Ⅳ.Essentials for Learning Shaolin Quan　015

第二章　少林拳基础技术技法　021

一、少林拳基本手型与步型　022

二、少林拳基本技法　032

Chapter 2　Basic Techniques and Skills in Shaolin Quan　021

Ⅰ.Basic Hand and Foot Techniques of Shaolin Quan　023

Ⅱ.Basic Techniques of Shaolin Quan　033

第三章　少林拳基础练习　051

一、面壁功　052

二、椅子桩　052

三、丁步桩　054

四、弓步斜行　054

五、马步单鞭 056
六、虚步挑掌 058
七、仆步切掌 060
八、歇步冲拳 060
九、转身推掌 062

Chapter 3 Practice of Basics in Shaolin Quan 051
Ⅰ.Wall-facing Practice 053
Ⅱ.Chair-shaped Half-squat Stance 053
Ⅲ.T-shaped Half-squat Stance 053
Ⅳ.Diagonal Bow Stance 055
Ⅴ.Horse Stance with Single Whip 057
Ⅵ.Empty Stance with Uplift Palm 057
Ⅶ.Flat Stance with Slicing Palm 059
Ⅷ.Rest Stance with Punch Fist 061
Ⅸ.Turning Body with Pushing Palm 061

第四章 少林拳套路 065
一、少林罗汉十八手 066
二、连环拳 086

Chapter 4 Shaolin Quan Routines 065
Ⅰ. Arhat Eighteen Hands 067
Ⅱ. Interlinked Fist 087

第五章　少林拳实战技法 115

一、罗汉十八手实战技法 116

二、连环拳实战技法 148

Chapter 5 Shaolin Quan Combating Skills 115

Ⅰ.Arhat Eighteen Hands in Actual Combat 117

Ⅱ.Interlinked Fist in Actual Combat 149

后　记 165

Epilogue 167

附录：中国历史年代简表 170

Appendix: A Brief Chronology of Chinese History 170

第一章

少林拳概述

Chapter 1

Overview of Shaolin Quan

一、少林寺与少林拳

谈到少林拳的起源，首先要从少林寺的创建说起。根据《魏书·释老志》记载:“又有西域沙门名跋陀，有道业，深为高祖所敬信。诏于少室山阴，立少林寺而居之，公给衣供。”其中的“高祖”是指北魏孝文帝，是孝文帝为了安置所敬仰的印度高僧跋陀尊者，在与都城洛阳相望的嵩山少室山北麓为其建造的居所，此时正是北魏太和十九年(公元495年），这也是少林寺创建的年份。

少林寺是世界著名的佛教寺院，是汉传佛教的禅宗祖庭，在中国佛教史上占有重要地位，被誉为“天下第一名刹”。少林拳源于少林寺，拳以寺名，故称少林拳，又称少林功夫，是中国武术中的代表拳种。少林拳是少林拳术和器械的总称，是历代少林寺僧与军事将士及民间武术家们相互交流、久经实践、共同研究的结晶，素有“天下功夫出少林，少林功夫甲天下”之说。

少林拳内容丰富、套路繁多，高达七百种以上。按性质大致可分为内功、外功、硬功、轻功、气功等。内功以练精气为主；外功、硬功多指锻炼身体某部分的猛力；轻功专练纵跳和超距；气功包括练气和养气。套路又分拳术、棍术、枪术、刀术、剑术、徒手对练、器械对练等。这些套路和软硬功夫，由于年代久远，散失很多。

二、少林拳的历史渊源

关于少林拳的源流，有人认为由南北朝时期的达摩或拓跋所创，后来经过专家学者研究，这种说法均经不起考证。不少学者认为，追溯少林拳的起源，要从僧稠说起。僧稠是少林寺第一个有史可考的武僧，其主持少林寺后，少林寺习武风气渐浓，从而逐渐形成了内容丰富的少林武术。

Ⅰ. The Shaolin Temple and Shaolin Quan

When discussing the origins of Shaolin quan, it is essential to start with the establishment of the Shaolin Temple. According to the *Book of Wei: The Record of Buddhism*, "There was a monk from the Western Regions named Batuo, who was deeply respected and trusted by Emperor Gaozu. By imperial decree, the Shaolin Temple was established in the north of Mount Shaoshi for him to reside in, and he was provided with clothing and supplies." In the text, "Emperor Gaozu" refers to Emperor Xiaowen of the Northern Wei Dynasty. Emperor Xiaowen built the residence for the revered Indian monk Batuo at the northern foot of Mount Shaoshi, facing the capital Luoyang, in the 19th year of the Taihe Era (495 AD) which is also the year the Shaolin Temple was founded.

The Shaolin Temple is a world-renowned Buddhist monastery and the ancestral home of Zen in Chinese Buddhism, occupying an important position in the history of Chinese Buddhism and known as "the foremost temple in China". Shaolin quan originates from the Shaolin Temple, named after the temple itself, also known as Shaolin kungfu, representing a typical type of martial arts in China. Shaolin quan encompasses both boxing techniques and weapon skills developed through mutual exchange, long-term practice and collective research by monks from the Shaolin Temple, generals and soldiers, and martial artists from the populace. Thus, it gives rise to the saying, "All martial arts in China originated from Shaolin, and Shaolin kungfu are supreme in China."

Shaolin quan is rich in content and includes a wide variety of routines, amounting to over seven hundred types. Broadly, these can be roughly categorized into internal skill, external skill, hard skill, light skill, *qi* skill and so on. Internal skill mainly focuses on cultivating vital internal energy; external skill and hard skill often refer to training specific parts of the body for explosive force; light skill specializes in vertical jumps and long-distance leaps; *qi* skill includes the practice and nourishment of breath. The routines further divide into boxing, cudgel, spear, sabre, and sword techniques; barehanded sparring; and armed sparring, among others. Many of these routines and techniques, both soft and hard ones, have been lost over time due to their ancient origins.

达摩（如图1-2-1所示），印度僧人，是中国佛教史上最富传奇色彩的人物。相传他“一苇渡江”，历经多重磨难，于北魏孝明帝孝昌三年(公元527年)，来到中国河南省嵩山少林寺，传授佛教禅宗，后人尊他为“禅宗初祖”。据传，菩提达摩坐禅面壁九年，由于长期静坐，看到弟子精神和肉体都容易困倦，同时经常受到猛兽威胁，便根据山林中虎跃、猴攀、鸟飞、虫爬等形态动作，并效法我国劳动人民锻炼身体的各种活动，初创了简单的健体技击术来研练。达摩初创的这些健身技击术虽然简单，却是少林寺优秀的强身养生术，对后世少林拳禅武合一理念的形成有着根源性的影响。因达摩在佛教禅宗中的贡献，后人假托其名研创出“达摩剑”“达摩杖”等系列传统少林武术套路。

图1-2-1
Fig. 1-2-1

僧稠（如图1-2-2所示），生于北魏太和四年(公元480年)，少林寺的第二任住持。唐人张鷟《朝野佥载》记载：“北齐稠禅师，邺人也，幼落发为沙弥。时辈甚众，每休暇，常角力腾趠为戏。……横塌壁行，自西至东凡数百步，又跃首至于梁数四。乃引重千钧，其拳捷骁武劲。”据此可以看出，他不仅博览佛经而且懂拳晓武，还精练兵器，擅长气功、轻功，能横塌墙行，跃首至梁，又善于研练健体延寿之术，在当时僧稠是一位著名的武术高手。

II. Historical Origins of Shaolin Quan

Regarding the origins of Shaolin quan, some have speculated that it was created during the Northern and Southern Dynasties by Bodhidharma or Tuoba. However, upon further examination by experts and scholars, such claims have not been substantiated. Many scholars believe that to trace the origins of Shaolin quan, one must start with Monk Sengchou. Sengchou was the first historically documented warrior monk of the Shaolin Temple. After he took charge of the Shaolin Temple, the practice of martial arts within the temple became increasingly prevalent, leading to the gradual formation of the rich martial arts tradition known as Shaolin kungfu.

Bodhidharma (As shown in Fig. 1-2-1), an Indian monk, is one of the most legendary figures in the history of Chinese Buddhism. It is said that he "crossed a river on a reed" and, after enduring numerous hardships, arrived at the Shaolin Temple on Mount Song in Henan Province in the third year of the Xiaochang Era (527 AD) during the reign of Emperor Xiaoming of the Northern Wei Dynasty. There, he taught Zen Buddhism, and later generations honored him as the "First Patriarch of Zen". Legend has it that Bodhidharma faced the wall in meditation for nine years. Due to the long periods of sitting, he noticed that his disciples easily became physically and mentally fatigued. They were also often threatened by wild beasts. Drawing inspiration from the movements of tigers leaping, monkeys climbing, birds flying, and insects crawling in the forest, and emulating the various physical activities practiced by the working people of the country, he created a set of simple physical exercises and fighting techniques. Although these initial health and combat techniques devised by Bodhidharma were simple, they became the foundation of excellent health and fitness practices at the Shaolin Temple. They significantly influenced the integration of Zen and martial arts in Shaolin quan for generations to come. In recognition of Bodhidharma's contributions to Zen Buddhism, later generations attributed the creation of some traditional Shaolin martial arts routines such as the Bodhidharma Sword (*Damo Jian*) and Bodhidharma Cane (*Damo Zhang*) to his name.

Sengchou (As shown in Fig. 1-2-2), born in the fourth year of the Taihe Era

图1-2-2

Fig. 1-2-2

福居，少林寺方丈，北宋初年（约公元961年）先后三次邀请全国十八家武林高手会于少林寺，进行武功技法交流，广泛吸取众家之长，最后汇集成册，整理出了一套拳谱，流传至今。据《少林寺拳谱秘抄》记载："宋太祖乾德元年（公元963年），福居指示弟子灵智、灵敏、灵丘等，将十八家武艺结合宋以前寺僧习武的经验，汇编成《少林拳谱》四十八卷。"

秋月，山西太原人，酷爱武术，精通气功，擅长剑术，凡过路侠客有一技之长者，即虚心求教，久之家徒四壁，后周游四方，以授徒传武为业，经李叟介绍与少林寺觉远和尚认识后，同住少林寺，每日共同演练和探讨少林武技，其间撰写了《五拳精要》一书，系统地阐述了龙、虎、豹、蛇、鹤五拳的特点和手、足、身、眼、步法以及五拳组合的练法。他在少林寺不仅将几十年的武艺精华和超人功夫毫不保留地传给寺僧，而且对寺内演练的某些套路增补了招式，使其结构严谨、风格独特、攻防兼备、利于实战，如罗汉十八手、行龙剑、五合拳、黑虎拳等。

紧那罗（如图1-2-3所示），据《少林寺志》记载，他是元末明初少林寺烧火做饭的和尚，俗名许那罗，河南偃师人。他对于刀法、枪法、棍棒法、剑戟、草镰等武艺十分纯熟。尤其善用双刀、双戟、草镰

of the Northern Wei Dynasty (480 AD), was the second abbot of the Shaolin Temple. Zhang Zhuo, a Tang Dynasty historian, recorded in *Anecdotes of the Court and the Commonality* that "Sengchou, a Zen master from the Northern Qi Dynasty, originally from Ye County, became a novice monk at a young age. Among his peers, he was extremely active. During leisure times, he often engaged in wrestling and jumping as play… He could traverse walls horizontally, moving from west to east for hundreds of steps, and then leap from the ground to beams four times in succession, pulling weights of a thousand catties with his strength. His punches were swift, fierce, and powerful." From this, it is evident that he was not only well-versed in Buddhist scriptures but also good at martial arts. He was proficient with weapons, excelled in *qi* skill and light skill, could move horizontally across walls, leap to beams, and was adept at practicing health and longevity techniques. At that time, Sengchou was a renowned martial arts master.

Fuju, the Abbot of the Shaolin Temple during the early Northern Song Dynasty (around 961 AD), invited martial arts masters from eighteen schools across the country to the Shaolin Temple on three occasions. These meetings facilitated the exchange of martial arts techniques, drawing extensively from the strengths of various schools, and culminating in the compilation of a set of manuals that have been passed down to the present day. According to *The Secret Shaolin Quan Manuals*, "In the first year of the Qiande Era under Emperor Taizu of the Song Dynasty (963 AD), Fuju directed his disciples Lingzhi, Lingmin, Lingqiu and others to integrate the martial arts of eighteen schools with the martial experience previously accumulated by the temple's monks before the Song Dynasty, resulting in the compilation of *The Shaolin Quan Manuals* in forty-eight volumes."

Qiuyue, a native of Taiyuan, Shanxi, who had a profound passion for martial arts and was skilled in *qi* and swords, eagerly learned from every expert he encountered. His dedication eventually led to his financial ruin. He later traveled extensively, dedicating his life to teaching martial arts. After being introduced to Monk Jueyuan of the Shaolin Temple, he lived there, spending his days in joint practice and discussion of Shaolin martial arts techniques. During this period, he completed *The Essentials of Five Boxing Styles*, which meticulously described the characteristics and training methods of the dragon, tiger, leopard,

和大棍等武器，流传于世的有《紧那罗兵法十五篇》。少林武僧尊称他为二辈爷，自古至今，他在少林寺僧人的心目中影响深远。自元代后，寺僧和民间武林诸士都尊其为“紧那罗王”，还有人称之为“少林棍法之祖”。

图1-2-3

Fig. 1-2-3

少林武术分为五大流派，有河南（嵩山）少林、福建少林、广东少林、峨嵋少林和武当少林，每派中又分为许多小派和门类，派别繁多。从地域上又可分为北少林和南少林两大流派。南派重拳，北派重腿。

三、少林拳的技法要领

少林拳在习练时对手法、眼法、身法、步法都有严格的要求。主要

snake, and crane boxing styles, including instructions on hand, foot, body, eye, and stance techniques, as well as the combined practice of these five types of boxing styles. He generously shared his extensive knowledge and remarkable skills with the monks within the Shaolin Temple, enriching some practiced routines with additional moves to ensure they were well-structured, uniquely styled, defensively and offensively balanced, and practical for combat situations, including techniques such as Arhat Eighteen Hands (*Luohan Shiba Shou*), Moving Dragon Sword (*Xinglong Jian*), Five-Harmony Fist (*Wuhe Quan*) and Black Tiger Fist (*Heihu Quan*).

Kinnara (As shown in Fig. 1-2-3), as chronicled in *The Records of the Shaolin Temple*, served as a cook at the temple during the late Yuan and early Ming periods. His lay name was Xu Naluo, and he came from Yanshi, Henan. He was highly proficient in various martial arts, including techniques for sabers, spears, sticks, halberds, and sickles. He was particularly adept at dual sabers, dual halberds, sickles, and large clubs. His teachings, encapsulated in *The Fifteen Chapters of Kinnara's Martial Techniques*, have been preserved through generations. Warrior monks of the Shaolin Temple have long esteemed him as a revered figure, affectionately referring to him as "Second Generation Master". His influence on the monks and the martial arts community of the Shaolin Temple has been profound and enduring. Since the Yuan Dynasty, he has been venerated as "King Kinnara" by monks and martial artists alike, with some also recognizing him as "The Ancestor of Shaolin Staff Fighting Techniques".

Shaolin martial arts are divided into five major schools: Henan (Songshan) Shaolin, Fujian Shaolin, Guangdong Shaolin, Emei Shaolin, and Wudang Shaolin. Each school further subdivides into many smaller sects and categories, making for a wide variety of traditions. Geographically, they can also be divided into two major factions: Northern Shaolin and Southern Shaolin. The Southern style emphasizes punches, while the Northern style focuses on kicks.

III. Key Techniques of Shaolin Quan

Shaolin quan has strict requirements for hand techniques, eyesight, body movement, and footwork during practice. The main techniques are as follows:

技法要领如下。

1. 手法迅猛

少林拳对手法要求“拳如流星”，要迅速、有力。所谓迅速不仅仅是挥拳的动作要快捷，同时要求手法、肩、肘、手腕的配合动作也要快速一致。

习练时要实现“拳如流星”，就必须做到肩、肘、手臂松活，实现节节贯穿，使肩、肘、腕各关节在运行时灵活顺畅。如，做“冲拳”时，起于梢节，肘相随，用肩催，拳走直线，用力通达，拧腰、顺肩，急速旋转手臂，力达拳面。

2. 眼睛明锐

少林拳对眼法的要求是“目似闪电”，要明快、眼光如炬。少林拳的眼光不是孤立的运用，而是要与动作相配合。大体可分为两类：第一类是随视，要求眼睛要跟随手的动作；第二类是注视，要做到“眼随视注”。要实现运动中手法像流星般迅速和眼随手动、手到眼到，就必须有闪电一样明快锐利的眼法变化。眼法变化既要与身体的动作紧密联系，又要与颈部活动密切相关。随着动作的变化，眼睛要做到左顾右盼、上下注视。眼法是表现动作意向和传神的关键，因此，眼法必须做到眼随手动、眼光如炬。

3. 身法灵活

习练少林拳时，身法与腰密切相关，因此，要求“腰如蛇形”，做到柔韧、灵活、自如。身法在少林拳中常常表现为闪、转、展、缩、弯等身体变化，这些变化多以腰为主。因此，身法要求“如蛇形”,一方面要求身法的变化不能程式化、固定化，要像蛇爬行那样蜿蜒起伏，灵活多变；另一方面对胸和腰要求具有较好的柔韧性，只有如此，动作才能表现出既柔顺又坚韧。

4. 步法稳固

少林拳对步法要求是“步赛粘”。意思是站立时要像脚步粘连在

1.Rapid and Powerful Punches

Shaolin quan demands that punches be "as swift as a meteor", meaning they must be quick and powerful. The speed refers not only to the swiftness of punching but also to the coordinated and rapid movements of hands, shoulders, elbows, and wrists.

To deliver the "meteor-like punch", practitioners must ensure that shoulders, elbows, and arms are relaxed and flexible, resulting in seamless connection through each section, while allowing shoulders, elbows, and wrists to move fluidly during execution. For instance, in a forward punch, the movement starts from the hand, followed by the elbow, driven by the shoulder, with the punch moving in a straight line and the force thoroughly exerted. The waist twists, the shoulder follows, and the arm rotates, ensuring the force is effectively delivered to the front of the fist.

2. Keen Eyesight

Shaolin quan requires the eyes to be as lightning, meaning they should be sharp and piercing. The use of eyes in Shaolin quan is not isolated but is meant to coordinate with movements. The requirements on eyesight can generally be divided into two categories: the first is to follow, meaning the eyes should follow the movement of hands; the second is to focus, which requires the eyes to follow and focus on the actions. To accomplish swift punches and the perfect coordination of eyes and hands, one must have eyesight as quick and sharp as lightning. The variation in eyesight must closely link with the movements of both body and neck. With the change of actions, the eyes should be able to quickly look left and right, up and down. Eyesight is key to expressing the intention of actions and conveying spirit; thus, it is essential that the eyesight is coordinated with the hands and is as illuminating as a torch.

3. Flexible Body Movements

In Shaolin quan, body movements are closely related to the waist, hence the requirement for the waist is to be like a snake, demonstrating flexibility, agility, and freedom. Body movements in Shaolin quan often manifest as dodging, turning, extending, retracting, bending, and other body changes. And they predominantly center around the waist. Thus, body movements should imitate those of a snake, implying that changes in body movements should not be rigid or fixed but undulating and flexible like the movement of a snake. On the other

土地上那样稳固。不受上肢、下肢和躯干活动的影响，还要给上肢、下肢和躯干灵活运动提供必要的稳固条件和基础保障。此外，步法还要轻便灵活。拳谚曰“步不稳则拳乱，步不快则拳慢”，生动地说出了步法在练习拳术时所起的作用。只有做到步法稳固、轻快，才能达到下盘稳定，动而不乱。以快速的步法催动拳速，步到拳到，达到上下协调一致。

5. 力要顺达

少林拳对劲力的要求是“力要顺达”。发力顺达是动作相互之间顺利衔接的必备条件，否则就会使动作僵硬、呆板，出现僵劲硬力，破坏动作连贯性与套路的节奏。要做到用力顺达，就必须从明 “三节”、懂“六合”入手。三节，从上肢来看，手为梢节，肘为中节，肩为根节；从下肢来看，脚为梢节，膝为中节，胯为根节。不同的动作有不同的用力顺序，如冲拳、推掌皆产生于梢节，蹬脚、弹踢则产生于根节。六合分内三合和外三合，心与意合、意与气合、气与力合，为内三合；肩与胯合、手与足合、肘与膝合为外三合。掌握好“三节”的发力顺序和“六合”的协调关系，动作才会通达流畅。

6. 功夫纯青

少林拳对技术的要求是“功宜纯”。这里的“功”是指少林拳的技术及运用技术的技能与技巧。“功宜纯”是指要求功夫像炉火一样纯青。虽说这是虚拟与夸张的比喻，但确实体现出对少林拳技术高质量的要求。要获得纯青的技术，首要的一条是在技术规范化的前提下不断地实践与探索，只有坚持习练，持之以恒，才能使体能与技能不断提高，使技艺不断升华，功夫与日俱增，逐渐达到理想的纯青境地。

hand, there is a high demand for flexibility in the chest and the waist, as flexibility is the key for these movements to exhibit both suppleness and resilience.

4. Stable Footwork

Shaolin quan demands that the footwork be as if glued, meaning that when standing, the feet should be as firmly attached to the ground as if glued. They should be unaffected by the movements of the upper limbs, lower limbs, and torso, while providing the necessary stability and foundational support for the flexible movements of these three parts. Furthermore, the footwork should also be light and agile. The adage "unsteady steps lead to disordered punches, slow steps lead to slow punches" vividly illustrates the role of footwork in practice. Only with stable, swift footwork can one achieve a stable lower stance and remain orderly despite motion. Quick footwork accelerates punch speed, with each step followed by a punch, achieving coordination and consistency between upper and lower body movements.

5. Smooth Delivery of Force

Shaolin quan requires that force should be smoothly delivered. The smooth delivery of force is essential for the seamless connection between movements; otherwise, it results in stiff, rigid movements that break the continuity and rhythm of movements and routines. Smooth delivery of force starts with understanding the three sections and grasping the six harmonies. The three sections, from the perspective of the upper limbs, are the hand (the tip), the elbow (the middle), and the shoulder (the root); and from the lower limbs, include the foot (the tip), the knee (the middle), and the hip (the root). Different movements have different sequences of force application. For instance, punches and palm pushes start from the tip, while kicks come from the root. The six harmonies are divided into the internal three harmonies (heart with intent, intent with *qi*, *qi* with force) and the external three harmonies (shoulders with hips, hands with feet, elbows with knees). Mastering the sequence of force in the three sections and the coordination of the six harmonies ensures movements are fluid and connected.

6. Proficiency in Skills

The requirement of Shaolin quan for the mastery of techniques is that the skills should be pure. Here, skills refer to both the techniques of Shaolin quan and the ability to apply these techniques skillfully. Pure skills mean the skill should be

四、学拳旨要

历代武术前辈和习练者，在长期的武术习练中，积累了许多丰富、宝贵的经验。提前知晓少林武术的特点，将来的功夫学习可以少走弯路，达到事半功倍的效果。

1. 拳打一条线

少林拳的基本套路练习中，步法的进退，身法的起、横、落、顺，其运动路线总的趋势基本上都是沿着直线进行的。两点之间，直线最短。真正的交手，双方之间无非几步之距，即能分出胜负。“拳打一条线”的运动特点，充分显示出了少林拳的快速、简洁、实用。直线作为最短距离，可以使人在最短时间、最佳时机来攻击对手。少林拳不练花架子，自然朴实，一切从实际出发，讲究“拳不华丽讲实用”，不强调外形的美观，只求技击的实用性，猛打能攻，硬取直上，追求以最佳时间、最佳战机、最佳距离、最佳手段来取得最理想的战术效果。当然，所谓的“拳打一条线”，其实只是从整体外形上而言的。实际上，在整体外形的“拳打一条线”中，已经包含了很多弧线、转折、迂回、翻转等技法，需要根据对手的情况不断变换招法，因地制宜，活学活用。

2. 拳打卧牛之地

这是说少林拳的练习和运用不受场地大小的限制，可随时随地地发挥其拳脚的威力。在广阔的场地上，可以练习运用少林拳；在很小的范围内，少林拳的进退转折、翻转腾跃、攻击防守，也照样可以施展出来。在小范围内练习少林拳，要求步子小、身法灵、动作活、速度快。由于少林拳主要是在深山中与寺院里练成的，长期的练习客观上受到了某种程度的限制，但却可以培养练习者身灵步活、声东击西的能力，培养练习者的突围能力，使其能够在短时间、短距离内施展拳脚，运用技术克敌制胜。

as refined as fire. Although this is a metaphorical exaggeration, it indeed reflects the high-quality demand of Shaolin quan techniques. Attainment of pure skills primarily involves continuous practice and exploration under the premise of standardized techniques. Only through persistent practice and perseverance can physical strength be improved continuously, skills be enhanced day by day, and the ideal state of purity be reached.

IV. Essentials for Learning Shaolin Quan

Generations of martial arts predecessors and practitioners have gathered a rich and valuable trove of experiences through long-term martial arts practice. Knowing the characteristics of Shaolin martial arts in advance can streamline future learning, yielding more results with less effort.

1. Punching along a Straight Line

In the practice of basic routines of Shaolin quan, the trend of movement routes, such as footwork and body movements, is generally along a straight line. As is known to all, the shortest distance between two points is a straight line. In actual combat, there are only a few steps between opponents. The characteristic of punching along a straight line fully demonstrates the speed, simplicity, and practicality of Shaolin quan. A straight line, being the shortest distance, allows one to attack the opponent with the shortest time and at the best moment. Shaolin quan does not focus on fancy moves, and it is natural and practical, emphasizing practicality over elegance, ignoring the aesthetic appearance, and focusing on the practicality of combat techniques. It aims to attack fiercely, move straight forward, and pursue the optimal tactical effects by pursuing the best time, opportunity, distance, and means. Obviously, the concept of "punching along a straight line" is only from an overall appearance perspective. In reality, within the straight-line punching, many techniques such as arcs, turns, detours, and reversals are included. It requires continuously changing tactics according to the opponent's situation, adapting to various circumstances, and applying knowledge flexibly.

2. Punching within a Limited Space

The practice and application of Shaolin quan are not limited by the size of the space, allowing its power to be unleashed anytime, anywhere. In a vast area,

3. 非曲非直，滚出滚入

少林拳手法运动的联合特点要求在出拳或出掌击打对方时，手臂直而不直、曲而不曲，这种方法在实战运用中既可以使速度更加快捷，同时也节省了来回运动时间。“身以滚而动，手以滚而出”，少林拳反对僵直拙力，在完成动作的一瞬间，依手臂的自然反弹力，使手臂形成曲非曲、直非直的态势，为继续攻防创造有利条件。“滚入滚出”是攻防技术的科学反映，在出拳时手臂要像螺旋一样旋转以袭击对方，滚入时旋动可增加攻击力，滚出时旋动有利于化解对方的来势力量。

4. 运气贵缓，用气贵急

“法是拳，气是力，练气行功，送去必用呼，接来必用吸，运气贵乎缓，用气贵乎急，气在先行，力在后随”，以及“力以柔而刚，气以运而实”。少林拳谱的这些表达，都充分表明少林拳对气运用的高度重视。少林拳流派的练气是以运使为效，以长吞短吐为功，以川流不息为主旨，以听气静虚为极致。少林拳派对于气的调节和运用，有其独到的见解，把它分成练气、养气、运气以及用气。运气练习时，多采用站桩、坐禅等，主要是以意念为主使，引领气血的运行，要求气血运行的速度，以缓慢运行为主，通达全身各处，达到气血流畅，运行自如；用力时，要求以意生力，协调快速调动气血，心意懂而招式出，意到气随，速于声响，以气催力。

5. 以声助威

少林拳的演练过程中还有一个发声特点，就是以声助威。通常演练者除了在套路结尾时随最后的动作发声“威”外，演练过程中也常有“呀”“噫”“哈”等不同的发声。这些发声源自腹腔，短促有力，吼声如雷，富有震撼性。

6. 动作迅猛，快速有力

少林拳要求刚健有力、迅速激烈，即所谓“起手连珠炮，拳打一气连”“使势千着，以快为先”。在套路演练过程中，要求几个动作连贯

one can practice and apply Shaolin quan; meanwhile, even in a small space, the footwork, turns, leaps, attacks, and defenses of Shaolin quan can still be performed. Practicing Shaolin quan in a confined space requires small steps, agile body movements, dynamic actions, and fast speed. As Shaolin quan is primarily developed in deep mountains and temples, its practice is mostly within limited space. However, it can cultivate the practitioner's agility, adaptability, and capability to surprise opponents, thus enhancing their ability to break through and effectively utilize techniques in a short time or within a limited space.

3. Remaining Neither Curved Nor Straight, and Rolling In and Rolling Out

The characteristic joint movement of punching in Shaolin quan requires the arms to be seemingly straight but not genuinely straight, seemingly curved but not genuinely curved when attacking an opponent with the fist or palm. This method not only enhances speed in practical combat but also saves time on unnecessary movements. Moving with rolling body, striking with rolling hands, Shaolin quan opposes rigid and clumsy force. At the moment of completing a movement, leveraging the natural rebound force of the arms creates a posture that is neither straight nor curved, setting up favorable conditions for continuous attack and defense. "Rolling in and rolling out" scientifically reflects the balance of attack and defense. In punching, the arms should attack the opponent by incorporating spiraling movement. Rotation during the rolling-in phase helps to increase the attacker' power, and rotation during the rolling-out stage aids in neutralizing the opponent's force.

4.Cultivating *Qi* Slowly and Releasing *Qi* Rapidly

"Fist is the means, and *qi* is the force. To train *qi* is to perform with power. One should exhale when sending out, inhaling when taking in. The movement of *qi* values slowness, while the release of *qi* underscores speed. *Qi* should lead and be followed by force." "Force combines softness with rigidity, and *qi* solidifies through movement." These expressions from manuals of Shaolin quan fully demonstrate the importance Shaolin quan places on the use of *qi*. The training of *qi* in the Shaolin school aims at effective delivery, taking long inhalations and short exhalations as the practice, a continuous flow as the theme, and tranquility and emptiness as the ultimate goal. The Shaolin school offers unique insights into

快速，一气呵成。少林拳虽然以刚为主，但同时也要求刚柔相济。“刚在他力前，柔在他力后”，动如风，站如钉；重如铁，轻如叶；守之如处女，犯之如猛虎；静则以逸待劳，动则使其无喘息之机等。

the regulation and application of *qi*, dividing it into the practice, nourishment, movement, and application of *qi*. In practicing *qi*, techniques such as standing postures and sitting meditation are often used, primarily focusing on using mind to guide the circulation of *qi* and blood. It demands a slow circulation speed to reach and nourish every part of the body, resulting in a smooth and free flow of *qi* and blood. In releasing force, it emphasizes generating power through mind, quickly and harmoniously mobilizing *qi* and blood, with moves performed swiftly and *qi* led by intent to drive force.

5. Boosting Morale with Shout

Another characteristic of Shaolin quan practice is the use of vocalizations to boost morale. Practitioners often shout "wei" at the end of a routine in addition to various shouts like "ya", "yi", and "ha" during practice. These vocalizations originate from the diaphragm, short and powerful, thunderous, and impactful.

6. Acting Swiftly and Powerfully

Swift and powerful actions are emphasized in Shaolin quan. This is known as "starting with a continuous burst of punches, striking continuously in one breath" and "exercising a thousand postures with speed as the priority". During routine practice, the movements should be continuous, rapid, seamless. While Shaolin quan primarily focuses on strength, it also emphasizes the balance between firmness and flexibility. "Firmness precedes the opponent's strength, flexibility follows behind". One should move like the wind yet stand firm like a nail; be heavy as iron or light as a leaf; defend like a virgin, and attack like a fierce tiger; remain still to await the opponent's exhaustion, and act swiftly to leave no opportunity for the opponent to recover.

第二章

少林拳基础技术技法

Chapter 2

Basic Techniques and Skills in Shaolin Quan

一、少林拳基本手型与步型

1. 基本手型

（1）拳

五指攥紧，拳面要平，拇指压于食指、中指第二指节上。

拳分为拳心、拳背、拳面、拳眼、拳轮。（如图2-1-1所示）

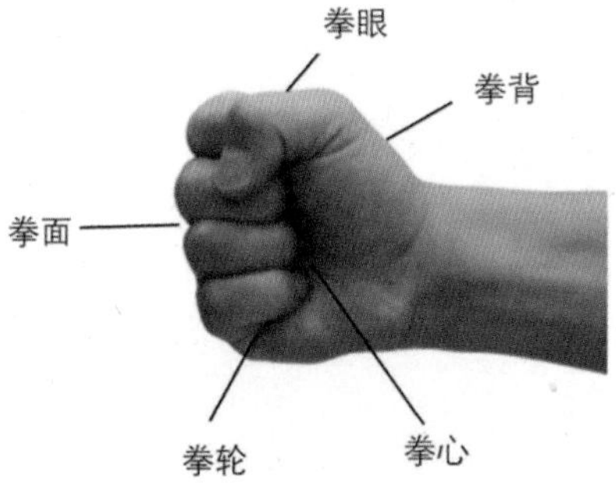

图2-1-1

Fig. 2-1-1

拳心：手心的一面。

拳背：手背的一面。

拳面：食指、中指、无名指和小指的第一节指骨相并形成的平面。

拳眼：拇指根部与食指相叠而成的螺旋形圆窝。

拳轮：小指一侧的螺旋圆窝。

（2）掌

柳叶掌:拇指内屈，其余四指伸直并拢向后伸张。（如图2-1-2所示）

八字掌:拇指伸直，虎口张开，其余四指伸直并拢向后伸张。

分指掌（透风掌）:五指用力分开，掌心微凹。

Ⅰ. Basic Hand and Foot Techniques of Shaolin Quan

1. Basic Hand Forms

(1) Fist

Clench the five fingers tightly, keep the front of the fist flat, and press the thumb on the second joints of the index and middle fingers.

The fist consists of the fist heart, fist back, fist front, fist eye, and fist wheel.(As shown in Fig. 2-1-1)

Fist heart: The palm side of the hand.

Fist back: The back of the hand.

Fist front: The flat surface formed by the first joints of the index, middle, ring, and little fingers.

Fist eye: The spiral cavity formed by the overlapping of the root of the thumb and the index finger.

Fist wheel: The spiral cavity of the fist on the side of the little finger.

(2)Palm

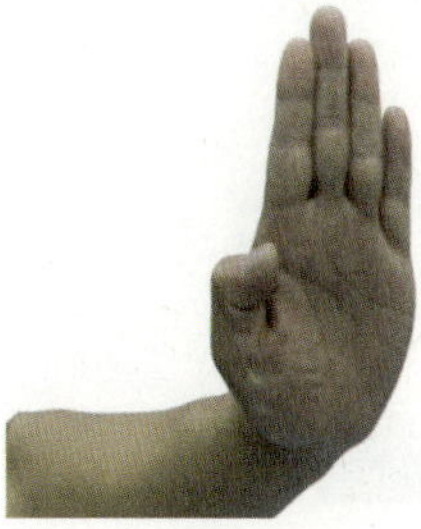

图2-1-2

Fig. 2-1-2

Willow Leaf Palm: Bend the thumb inward, while keeping the other four fingers straightened, put together, and extended backward.(As shown in Fig. 2-1-2)

Eight-character Palm: Straighten the thumb. Keep the space between the thumb and index finger open. Make sure the other four fingers are straightened, put together, and extended backward.

Split Finger Palm (also known as Wind-piercing Palm): Spread the five fingers apart forcefully, with the palm slightly concave.

（3）勾

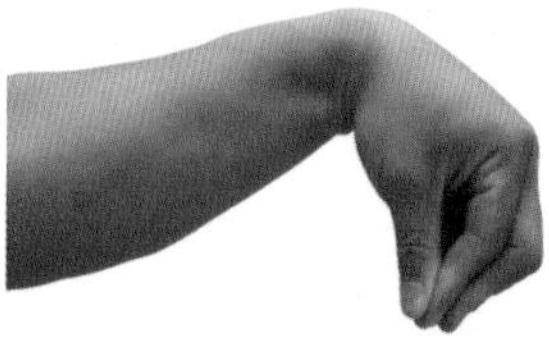

图2-1-3
Fig.2-1-3

屈腕，拇指与食指、中指撮拢，无名指、小指依次内屈。（如图2-1-3所示）

（4）爪

五指有力分开，第二、三节指骨弯曲，第一节指骨尽量向手背的一面伸张，掌心凸出。（如图2-1-4所示）

（5）指

中指与食指自然伸直，其余三指屈于手心，拇指压在无名指第一指节上。（如图2-1-5所示）

图2-1-5
Fig. 2-1-5

2. 基本步型

（1）弓步

动作说明：

左脚向前一大步（约为本人脚长的四至五倍），脚尖微微内扣，左腿屈膝半蹲（大腿接近水平），膝盖与脚尖垂直，右腿挺膝伸直，右脚

(3) Hook

Bend the wrist, gather the thumb with the index and middle fingers, while the ring and little fingers curl inward sequentially.(As shown in Fig. 2-1-3)

(4) Claw

Spread the five fingers apart forcefully. Bend the second and third joints of the fingers, extend the first joints of the fingers as much as possible toward the back of the hand, with the palm protruding.(As shown in Fig. 2-1-4)

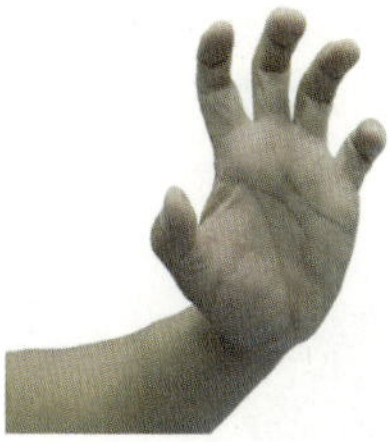

图2-1-4
Fig.2-1-4

(5) Finger

Extend the index and middle fingers naturally straight, while curling the remaining three fingers toward the palm. Press the thumb on the first joint of the ring finger.(As shown in Fig. 2-1-5)

2.Basic Stances

(1) Bow Stance

Movement Description:

Take a big step forward with the left foot (approximately four to five times the length of a foot), slightly turn the toes inward, and bend the left knee into a half-squat position (with the thigh being close to horizontal), making the knee vertical with the toes. Extend the right leg, with the knee being straight, the right foot toes pointing slightly inward (angled forward), and both feet being flat on the ground (approximately three and a half times the length of a foot). Keep the upper body facing forward, eyes looking straight ahead, and clench hands into fists at the waist with the fist hearts facing upward. When the right leg is bent, it is called the right bow stance; and when the left leg is bent, it is termed the left bow stance. (As shown in Fig. 2-1-6)

尖内扣（斜向前方），两脚全脚掌着地（两脚间距三脚半左右）。上体正对前方，眼睛向前平视，两手抱拳于腰间，拳心向上。弓右腿为右弓步，弓左腿为左弓步。（如图2-1-6所示）

动作要点：

前腿弓，后腿绷；挺胸、塌腰、沉髋，前脚尖同后脚跟呈一条直线。

图2-1-6
Fig.2-1-6

（2）马步

动作说明：

两脚平行开立（约为本人脚长的三倍），脚尖正对前方，屈膝半蹲，膝盖不超过脚尖，大腿接近水平，全脚掌着地，身体重心落于两腿之间。两手抱拳于腰间，拳心向上。（如图2-1-7所示）

动作要点：

挺胸、塌腰、脚跟外蹬、脚尖稍内扣。

（3）仆步

动作说明：

左右两脚开立，右腿屈膝全蹲，大腿和小腿紧靠，臀部接近小腿，右脚全脚掌着地，脚尖和膝关节外展；左腿挺直平仆，脚尖内扣，全脚

Key Points:

Bow the front leg. Keep the back leg straight, the chest up, the waist down, and the hips sunk. Make sure the front toes align with the back heel in a straight line.

(2) Horse Stance

Movement Description:

Stand with the feet parallel and apart (approximately three times the length of a foot), with the toes facing forward. Bend the knees into a half-squat position, ensuring they do not extend beyond the toes, with the thighs close to horizontal and the entire soles of the feet on the ground. Center the body's weight between the two legs. Clench the hands into fists at the waist, with the fist hearts facing upward (As depicted in Fig. 2-1-7).

Key Points:

Push out the chest, sink the waist, press down on heels, and turn the toes slightly inward.

图2-1-7

Fig.2-1-7

(3) Flat Stance

Movement Description:

Stand with the feet apart. Bend the right knee into a full squat, with the thigh and calf close together, and the buttocks near the calf. Ensure the entire sole of the right foot touches the ground, with toes and the right knee pointing outward. Keep the left leg straight and flat, with toes pointing inward and the entire sole on the ground. Clench the hands into fists at the waist, with the fist hearts facing upward. Gaze straight toward the left. When the left leg is extended, it is referred to as the left flat stance; and when the right leg is extended, it is called the right

着地。两手抱拳于腰间，拳心向上。眼睛向左方平视。仆左腿为左仆步，仆右腿为右仆步。（如图2-1-8所示）

动作要点：

挺胸、塌腰、沉髋，两脚全脚掌着地。

图2-1-8
Fig.2-1-8

（4）虚步

动作说明：

两脚前后开立，右脚外展45度，屈膝半蹲；左脚脚跟离地，脚面绷直，脚尖稍微内扣，虚点地面，膝盖微屈。重心落在后腿上。两手叉腰，眼睛向前平视。左脚在前为左虚步，右脚在前为右虚步。（如图2-1-9所示）

动作要点：

挺胸、塌腰、沉髋，虚实分明。

（5）歇步

动作说明：

左（右）脚在前，右（左）脚在后，两腿交叉靠拢屈膝全蹲，左（右）脚掌全着地，脚尖外展；右（左）脚前脚掌着地，右（左）膝盖贴近左（右）膝窝处。两手抱拳于腰间，拳心向上。眼睛向左前方平视。左脚在前为左歇步，右脚在前为右歇步。（如图2-1-10所示）

flat stance. (As depicted in Fig. 2-1-8)

Key Points:

Push out the chest, tuck in the waist, sink the hips, and keep the soles of both feet on the ground.

(4) Empty Stance

Movement Description:

Stand with the feet apart. Position the left foot in front of the right. Turn the right foot outward by 45 degrees and bend the knee into a half-squat. Lift the heel of the left foot off the ground, keeping the instep taut and the toes slightly inward, touching the ground lightly with the tip of the foot, and bending the knee slightly. The weight should be on the back leg. Place both hands on the wasit, and gaze straight ahead. When the left foot is positioned in front, it is called the left empty stance, and when the right foot is positioned in front, it is termed the right empty stance. (As shown in Fig. 2-1-9)

Key Points:

Push out the chest, lower the waist, sink the hips, and make a clear distinction between the solid and the empty stances.

图2-1-9

Fig.2-1-9

(5) Rest Stance

Movement Description:

With the left (right) foot in front and the right (left) foot behind, form a crossed stance. Bend the knees, lowering the body into a full squat. The enrie sole of the left (right) foot is flat on the ground with toes pointing outward; the ball of the right (left) foot touches the ground, and the right (left) knee stays close to the left (right) knee pit. Clench the hands into fists at the waist, with the fist

动作要点：

上身保持正直，两腿并拢夹紧，保持身体重心的平衡，臀部可坐在后脚跟。

图2-1-10

Fig.2-1-10

（6）蹲桩步

①椅子桩

动作说明：

两脚并拢，两腿屈膝半蹲，大腿接近水平，全脚掌着地。

动作要点：

两腿贴紧，双脚全脚掌着地，保持平衡，头正、颈直、立腰、直背。

②丁步桩

动作说明：

两脚全脚掌着地，前后并拢，一脚脚尖靠在另一脚内侧脚弓处，两腿屈膝下蹲，大腿接近水平。（如图2-1-11所示）

动作要点：

两腿前后并紧，双脚全脚掌着地，保持平衡，头正、颈直、立腰、直背。

hearts facing upward. Gaze straight ahead toward the left. When the left foot is positioned in front, it is called the left rest stance, and when the right foot is positioned in front, it is termed the right rest stance. (As shown in Fig. 2-1-10)

Key Points:

Keep the upper body upright, and the legs close together and tight to maintain the balance of the body. Rest the buttocks on the heel of the back foot.

(6) Half-squat Stance

①Chair-shaped Half-Squat Stance

Movement Description:

Keep the legs together, with knees bent into a half-squat, thighs being nearly horizontal, and the entire soles of the feet touching the ground.

Key Points:

Keep the legs close, with the entire soles of both feet flat on the ground to maintain balance. Hold the head straight, the neck aligned, the spine upright, and the back straight.

②T-shaped Half-Squat Stance

Movement Description:

Keep the entire soles of both feet flat on the ground, with heels close to each other. The toes of one foot rest against the inner arch of the other foot. Bend both legs in a half-squat, with thighs nearly horizontal. (As shown in Fig. 2-1-11)

Key Points:

Keep both legs together from front to back, with the entires soles of the feet flat on the ground to maintain balance. Hold the head straight, the neck aligned, the spine upright, and the back straight.

图2-1-11

Fig.2-1-11

（7）并步

动作说明：

上身直立，两腿屈膝并拢，全脚掌着地，目视前方。（如图2-1-12所示）

动作要点：

两膝贴紧，双脚全脚掌着地，头正、颈直、立腰、直背。

图2-1-12
Fig.2-1-12

二、少林拳基本技法

1. 少林拳基本手法

（1）抢手

动作说明：

双掌手心向上，从腰间向前上方插出，力达指尖。

（2）搂手

动作说明：

双手侧立，手背均向外，右手高，左手低，双臂呈弧形向同侧方向搂出。

(7) Squat Stance

Movement Description:

Keep the upper body erect with both legs bent at the knees and together. Ensure the entire soles of both feet are flat on the ground and gaze forward. (As shown in Fig. 2-1-12)

Key Points:

Keep the knees close together and the entire soles of both feet on the ground. Hold the head straight, the neck aligned, the waist erect, and the back straight.

Ⅱ. Basic Techniques of Shaolin Quan

1. Basic Hand Techniques of Shaolin Quan

(1) Thrusting Hands

Movement Description:

With both palms facing upward, thrust them forward and upward from the waist, directing the force through to the fingertips.

(2)Brushing Hands

Movement Description:

Stand with the arms at body sides and the backs of hands facing outward. Position the right hand higher than the left, and extend both arms toward the same direction in an arc as if to brush.

(3) Cloud Hands

Movement Description:

Position both hands in front of the chest, with the left hand above the right. Each hand makes a circular motion over the head, completing one full rotation. Following the rotation, clench the hands into fists and hold them at the waist.

(4) Dancing Flower Hands

Movement Description:

With the bases of the palms close to each other, twist the palms in either a clockwise or counterclockwise direction, mimicking the motion of entwining flowers.

（3）云手

动作说明：

两手相对于胸前，左手在上，两手依次在头顶上方盘旋一周后变拳抱于腰间。

（4）舞花手

动作说明：

两掌根相对交叉，逆时针或顺时针绞花。

（5）十字手

动作说明：

双手变掌，两手手腕于胸前交叉，指尖朝上，向前推出。

2. 少林拳基本拳法

（1）抱拳

动作说明：

两臂垂直上提，同时两手变拳抱于腰间，拳心向上。

动作要点：

两臂上提要快速、有力。

（2）冲拳

动作说明：

挺胸、收腹、直腰，左拳从腰间向内旋臂向前快速击出，拳心向下。紧接不停，乘前冲之势，左拳借反弹力回收，使臂保持微屈，拳眼向上。练习时左右拳可交替进行。

动作要点：

冲拳迅猛有力，冲拳时内旋臂成平拳，定势时外旋臂微回收成立拳。腿、腰、肩协调发力。

（3）抄拳

动作说明：

右手臂微屈，右拳自下向前上方抄起击打，拳背向前，力达拳面。

(5) Cross Hands

Movement Description:

Change both hands into palms, cross the wrists in front of the chest with fingertips pointing upward, and push forward.

2.Basic Fist Techniques of Shaolin Quan

(1) Holding Fists

Movement Description:

Raise both arms vertically; meanwhile clench both hands into fists and hold them at the waist, with the fist hearts facing upward.

Key Points:

Raise both arms swiftly and forcefully.

(2) Thrusting Fist

Movement Description:

Puff out the chest, tuck in the abdomen, and keep the back straight. Thrust the left fist forward from the waist with an inward rotation of the arm, while keeping the fist heart facing down. Without pause, leverage the momentum of the forward thrust to retract the left fist with the rebound force, while keeping the arm slightly bent and the fist eye facing upward. During practice, alternate between the left and right fists.

Key Points:

Thrust a fist swiftly and forcefully. When doing a thrusting fist, rotate the arm inward with the fist back upworad. Upon completion, slightly retract with an outward rotation to keep the fist eye upward. The legs, waist, and shoulders should coordinate with each other to generate force.

(3) Scooping Fist

Movement Description:

Bend the right arm slightly and scoop the right fist upward from below toward the upper front. Position the fist back to face forward and direct the force toward the fist front. During practice, alternate between the left and right fists.

Key Points:

When scooping up a fist, ensure that the fist does not rise above chest level.

练习时左右拳可交替进行。

动作要点：

拳抄起时高不过胸。

（4）撑拳

动作说明：

拳肘相并，屈臂从胸前向前向后侧击出，双臂成弧形，拳心向下，拳眼相对，力达拳轮。

动作要点：

手臂与肩相平。

（5）栽拳

动作说明：

臂由屈到伸，自上向下或由前向下栽。速度要快，前臂内旋，拳眼向内，臂伸直或微屈，力达拳面。练习时，左右可交替进行。

动作要点：

屈臂上勾，腰臂协调用力完成。

（6）架拳

动作说明：

右拳向下、向左、向上经头前向右上方划弧形架起，拳眼向下，眼看左方，练习时，左右可交替进行。

动作要点：

松肩，肘微屈，前臂内旋。

（7）劈拳

动作说明：

右拳经腹前向下、向左运行，向上经头前上方向右侧平劈，拳眼向上。练习时左右拳可交替进行。

动作要点：

拳与肩同高，臂微屈，力达拳轮，快速有力。动作过程中，眼随拳转。

(4) Supporting Fist

Movement Description:

Position the fist opposite the elbow of the other arm. With the arms bent, punch forward and backward from the chest. The arms form an arc, with the fist hearts facing downward and the fist eyes facing each other. The force is directed through to the fist wheels.

Key Points:

Ensure the arms are level with the shoulders.

(5) Plunging Fist

Movement Description:

Transition the arm from a bent to an extended position, plunging it downward either from above or front. The action should be quick, with the forearm rotating inward, the fist eye facing inward, and the arm either fully extended or slightly bent to direct force toward the fist front. During practice, alternate between the left and right fists.

Key Points:

Bend the arm and coordinate the waist and the arm to complete the action.

(6) Upholding Fist

Movement Description:

Direct the right fist downward, to the left, then upward and hold it toward the upper right in an arc over the head, with the fist eye facing downward. Gaze toward the left. During practice, alternate between the left and right fists.

Key Points:

Relax the shoulder, bend the elbow slightly, and rotate the forearm inward.

(7) Chopping Fist

Movement Description:

Direct the right fist downward and to the left across the front of the abdomen. Chop toward the right across the front of the head, with the fist eye facing upward. During practice, alternate between the left and right fists.

Key Points:

Keep the fist level with the shoulder, the arm slightly bent, and the force concentrated in the fist wheel. The action should be swift and powerful. Throughout the movement, the eyes should follow the fist.

（8）**贯拳**

动作说明：

右拳从腰间向前、向内旋臂呈弧形摆至面前，高与眼平，拳眼向下。练习时左右可交替进行。

动作要点：

臂呈弧形，弧线摆动，腰臂协调用力，力达拳面。

（9）**截把拳**

动作说明：

右臂屈90度于胸前，手心向上，左臂屈臂于右手前方，手心向上，两手同时变拳，右拳向后向下旋转，同时左拳向前向上旋转挑出，右拳在前、左拳在后，双拳拳心向下。

动作要点：

双臂旋转有力，协调发力。

（10）**反背拳**

动作说明：

拳于胸前，拳背向前，拳心向后，以肘为轴向前弹击。

动作要点：

发力迅速，力达拳背。

3. 少林拳基本掌法

（1）**推掌**

动作说明：

左掌从腰间内旋臂向前推出。接着迅速趁前推反弹力微回收，使左臂保持微屈，力达掌根或掌外沿，掌指向上。练习时左右掌可交替进行。

动作要点：

挺胸、收腹、直腰。推掌要快速有力，有寸劲；同时还要做好拧腰、顺肩、沉腕、翘掌等动作。

(8) Swinging Fist

Movement Description:

Swing the right fist in an arc from the waist forward to the front of the face while rotating the forearm inward. The fist reaches the eye level with the fist eye facing downward. During practice, alternate between the left and right fists.

Key Points:

The arm forms an arc, swinging in an arc trajectory. Coordinate the waist and arm to ensure the force is delivered through to the fist front.

(9) Intercepting Fist

Movement Description:

Bend the right arm at a 90-degree angle in front of the chest with the palm facing upward. Bend the left arm in front of the right hand, with the palm also facing upward. Clench both hands into fists at the same time; the right fist rotates backward and downward while the left fist rotates forward and upward, thrusting out, with the right fist being in front, the left fist being behind and the fist hearts facing downward.

Key Points:

Rotate the arms forcefully and coordinate the exertion of force.

(10) Back Fist

Movement Description:

Position the fist in front of the chest, with the fist back facing forward and the fist heart facing backward. Strike forward with the elbow as the pivot.

Key Points:

Strike swiftly. Ensure the force reaches the fist back.

3.Basic Palm Techniques of Shaolin Quan

(1) Pushing Palm

Movement Description:

Push the left palm forward from the waist while rotating the arm inward. Then, retract the palm slightly with the rebound force, keeping the left arm slightly bent. Direct the force either to the base or to the outer edge of the palm, with the fingers facing upward. During practice, alternate between the left and right palms.

（2）插掌

动作要领：

手臂提起，掌与胸平，臂由屈到伸，直腕向下（向前）插掌。

动作要点：

动作快速，力达指尖。

（3）砍掌

动作说明：

右拳变掌，屈臂至左胸前，掌指向上，掌心向左。目视左方。紧接不停，右掌向右挥砍，掌心向下，臂微屈，力达掌外沿。目视右掌方向。练习时左右手可交替进行练习。

动作要点：

动作快速，腰、臂发力协调一致。

（4）按掌

动作说明：

自上向下按，手心向下，力达掌心。

动作要点：

动作快速、有力。

（5）架掌

动作说明：

掌心向上，屈臂架于额前上方约15厘米处。

动作要点：

架掌迅速有力，力达上臂。

（6）扳掌

动作说明：

屈臂内收，掌经胸前，以肘关节为轴向前弹击。五指自然分开，掌心向内，力达掌背。

Key Points:

Push out the chest, pull in the abdomen, and straighten the waist. The action should be quick, forceful, and full of short-range explosive power. Meanwhile, pay attention to additional actions such as twisting the waist, aligning the shoulders, sinking the wrist, and tilting the palm.

(2) Thrusting Palm

Movement Description:

Raise the arm and position the palm at chest level, transitioning the arm from a bent to an extended position. With the wrist being straight, thrust the palm downward (forward).

Key Points:

The action should be swift. Direct the force through to the fingertips.

(3) Chopping Palm

Movement Description:

Unfurl the right fist into an open palm. Bend the arm and stop it at the left side of the chest with the fingers facing upward and the palm facing the left. Gaze toward the left. In a seamless transition, sweep the right palm outward to the right in a chopping motion, with the palm facing downward, the arm being slightly bent, and the force being concentrated at the outer edge of the palm. Gaze at the direction of the right palm. During practice, alternate between the left and right hands.

Key Points:

The action should be swift, with the waist and the arm coordinating seamlessly to exert force.

(4) Pressing Palm

Movement Description:

Press the palm downward from above, with the palm facing downward and the force delivered to the center of the palm.

Key Points:

The action should be swift and forceful.

(5) Framing Palm

Movement Description:

With the palm facing upward, bend the arm and position the palm approximately 15 centimeters above the forehead.

动作要点：

屈臂自然，力达掌背。

（7）撩掌

动作说明：

由下向前屈臂外旋，小指、无名指、中指、食指直指向上撩出。

动作要点：

各关节协调一致，力达掌根。

（8）切掌

动作说明：

俯掌沿另一臂下方向前切出，力达掌外沿。分下切、单切和双切。

动作要点：

切掌迅速有力，力达掌外沿。

4. 少林拳基本肘法

（1）顶肘

动作说明：

屈肘握拳，手心向下，肘尖前顶或侧顶，力达肘尖。

动作要点：

顶肘时拧腰发力，力达肘尖。

（2）盘肘

动作说明：

手臂平举，拳心向下，前臂由外向内盘肘。

动作要点：

盘肘拧腰发力，力达肘尖。

（3）架肘

动作说明：

屈臂外旋上举，拳心向前上方或正下方，屈臂90度置于额前，高不过头。

Key Points:

The action should be swift and powerful. Direct the force through to the upper arm.

(6) Wrenching Palm

Movement Description:

Bend the arm inward, move the palm in front of the chest, and flick the palm forward with the elbow joint as the pivot. Spread the five fingers apart, with the palm facing inward. Direct the force through to the back of the palm.

Key Points:

Bend the arm naturally and direct the force through to the back of the palm.

(7) Uppercut Palm

Movement Description:

Swing the palm forward from below, while bending the arm and rotating it forward, with the little finger, the ring finger, the middle finger, and the index finger extending straight upward.

Key Points:

All joints should work in coordination. Direct the force through to the base of the palm.

(8) Slicing Palm

Movement Description:

With the palm facing downward, slice it forward along the underside of the other arm, ensuring the force reaches the outer edge of the palm. Variations include the downward slice, single slice, and double slice.

Key Points:

The action should be swift and forceful. Direct the force through to the outer edge of the palm.

4. Basic Elbow Techniques in Shaolin Quan

(1) Thrusting Elbow

Movement Description:

Bend the elbow and clench the hand into fist, with the palm facing downward. Thrust the elbow forward or to the side, concentrating the force at the tip of the elbow.

动作要点：

架肘迅速有力，力达前臂。

（4）格肘（里格、外格）

动作说明：

前臂上屈，手心向里，力在前臂，向内横拨为里格，向外横拨为外格。

动作要点：

格肘迅速、拧腰发力。

（5）横击肘

动作说明：

肘关节屈，弧形向前，屈臂平击，力达肘尖和前臂外侧。

动作要点：

拧腰击肘，力达前臂。

5. 少林拳基本步法

（1）上步

动作说明：

一脚向前上一步，或两脚轮流向前上步，步大者称大步，步小者称小步，上半步者称半步。

动作要点：

上步要轻快，不拖泥带水。

（2）退步

动作说明：

也称倒步。脚向后退一步，或两脚轮流向后退步。用于退或转向。两只脚同时离地，向前或向后跳一步。

动作要点：

退步要迅速，不瞻前顾后。

Key Points:

Twist the waist to generate power while thrusting the elbow. Ensure the force reaches the tip of the elbow.

(2) Coiling Elbow

Movement Description:

Raise the arm to shoulder level, with the fist heart facing downward. Coil the forearm from outside to inside.

Key Points:

Twist the waist to generate force when coiling the elbow. Ensure the force reaches the tip of the elbow.

(3) Framing Elbow

Movement Description:

Bend the arm, rotate it outward, and lift it upward with the fist heart facing either upward or directly downward. Bend the arm at a 90-degree angle and position it in front of the forehead, not higher than the head.

Key Points:

The action should be swift and powerful. Direct the force through to the forearm.

(4) Blocking Elbow

Movement Description:

Bend the forearm upward with the palm facing inward and concentrate the force in the forearm. When the elbow strikes horizontally inward, it is called "inside blocking", and when the elbow strikes horizontally outward, it is called "outside blocking".

Key Points:

The action should be swift, with force generated by twisting the waist.

(5) Horizontal Strike Elbow

Movement Description:

Bend the elbow and move it forward in an arc motion. Strike horizontally with the bent arm. Ensure the force reaches the tip of the elbow and the outside of the forearm.

Key Points:

When striking with the elbow, twist the waist. Ensure the force reaches the

（3）偷步

动作说明：

也称插步。指两腿错步站立，一腿屈膝，全脚掌着地，脚尖外展；另一腿伸直后插，脚前掌着地，身体向前腿同侧方向扭转，并稍前倾。

动作要点：

后插步时腰腿要协调一致，一步到位。

（4）过步

动作说明：

步法术语。指盖步、盖跳步、倒插步等移动脚，超越支撑腿的步法。

动作要点：

过渡性步法，过步要迅速。

（5）击步

动作说明：

上体前倾，后脚离地提起，前脚随即蹬地前纵。在空中时，后脚向前碰击前脚。落地时，后脚先落，前脚后落。眼睛向前平视。

动作要点：

跳起在空中时，要保持上体正直并侧对前方。

（6）跳步

动作说明：

右脚提膝前摆，脚尖外展。左脚用力蹬地，使身体腾空。右脚先落地，左脚随后向前落步。如此可重复进行练习。

动作要点：

换跳要轻灵快速，腾空不可过高。

（7）垫步

动作说明：

身体重心移至左腿，两腿微屈，右脚抬起。右脚落于左脚内侧，左

forearm.

5. The Basic Step Techniques of Shaolin Quan

(1) Advancing Step

Movement Description:

Take a step forward with one foot, or step forward alternately with both feet. A large step is known as a "big step", a small step as a "small step", and a step covering half the distance as a "half step".

Key Points:

Advancing step should be quick and smooth, without any dragging or sluggishness.

(2) Retreating Step

Movement Description:

This type of step is also known as backing step. Take a step back with one foot, or step baceward alternately with both feet. It is taken to retreat or turn around. Both feet leave the ground simultaneously for a forward or backward jump.

Key Points:

The action should be swift. Do not hesitate.

(3) Sneaking Step

Movement Description:

This type of movement is also known as the "inserting step". Stand with the legs staggered: one leg is bent, with the entire sole of the foot flat on the ground and the toes pointing outward, while the other leg is extended back, resting on the ball of the foot. The body twists toward the side of the front leg and leans slightly forward.

Key Points:

When performing the backward inserting step, the waist and legs must coordinate smoothly and reach the position in one movement.

(4) Transitional Step

Movement Description:

A terminology in step techniques. This refers to the action of moving one foot beyond the supporting leg, as seen in maneuvers like the cover step, the cover jump step, and the inverted step.

脚向前上步呈预备姿势。此步法可连续进行练习。

动作要点：

右脚落地的同时左脚上步，动作连贯，进步时身体不腾空。

Key Points:

A transitional step technique. The action should be swift.

(5) Striking Step

Movement Description:

Lean the upper body forward, lift the rear foot off the ground, and then thrust the front foot forward in a lunge. While in the air, the rear foot strikes forward against the front foot. Upon landing, the rear foot lands first, followed by the front foot. Gaze straight ahead.

Key Points:

When jumping in the air, maintain an upright upper body and face sideways toward the front.

(6) Jump Step

Movement Description:

Lift the right knee and poistion the right foot in front, with the toes pointing outward. Push the ground with the left foot forcefully to propel the body into the air. The right foot lands first, followed by the left foot stepping forward. Repeat this sequence during practice.

Key Points:

The switch between jumps should be light and quick, avoiding excessive height.

(7) Shifting Step

Movement Description:

Shift your body weight onto the left leg, keep both legs slightly bent, and lift the right foot. Position the right foot inside next to the left foot, while the left foot steps forward into a ready position. This step can be practiced repeatedly for proficiency.

Key Points:

As the right foot touches down, step up simultaneously with the left foot, ensuring the movement is fluid. When advancing, the body does not leave the ground.

第三章

少林拳基础练习

Chapter 3

Practice of Basics in Shaolin Quan

学好少林拳基本功，不但可以帮助初学者尽快掌握和提高技术，而且对发展腰、腿、臂等身体各部位的柔韧性和力量，增强身体和心理素质，都有着积极的作用。现就少林拳基础练习介绍如下。

一、面壁功

动作说明：

两腿交叉，屈膝盘坐，两手分别扶于膝关节处，或两掌相叠，手心向上，放于腹前，两目垂帘。（如图3-1-1所示）

动作要点：

上体正直，全身放松，排除杂念，气沉丹田（注：位于下腹部脐下的位置）。

图3-1-1
Fig. 3-1-1

二、椅子桩

动作说明：

两脚并拢，屈膝半蹲，大腿成水平，两臂自然前伸，两掌掌心向下。（如图3-2-1所示）

Mastering the basics of Shaolin quan not only aids beginners in quickly acquiring and enhancing their techniques but also plays a positive role in developing flexibility and strength in various body parts such as the waist, legs, and arms, as well as in boosting physical and psychological qualities. An introduction to the basics of Shaolin quan is as follows.

Ⅰ. Wall-facing Practice

Movement Description:

Cross the legs, bend the knees, and sit in a lotus position. Place each hand on the knee joints, or overlap the two palms, facing upward, and rest them in front of the abdomen with the eyes closed. (As shown in Fig. 3-1-1)

Key Points:

Keep the upper body straight, relax the entire body, clear the mind of distractions, and sink the breath to the *dantian* area (Note: the area located below the navel in the lower abdomen).

Ⅱ. Chair-shaped Half-squat Stance

Movement Description:

Stand with the feet together, bend the knees into a half-squat position so that the thighs are parallel to the ground. Extend both arms naturally forward, with the palms facing downward. (As shown in Fig. 3-2-1)

Key Points:

Keep the upper body straight, relax the entire body, clear the mind of distractions, and concentrate the energy.

Ⅲ. T-shaped Half-squat Stance

Movement Description:

Bend both knees into a half-squat position, with the entire sole of the right foot on the ground and the toes of the left foot touching the ground next to the inside of the right foot. Bend the right arm at the elbow, and hold it in front of

动作要点：

上体正直，全身放松，排除杂念，精力集中。

图3-2-1
Fig.3-2-1

图3-2-1
Fig.3-2-1

三、丁步桩

动作说明：

两腿屈膝半蹲，右脚全脚着地，左脚脚尖点地于右脚内侧。右臂屈肘，竖靠于右肩前方，拳心朝后。左拳垂直向下插至左脚外踝骨上方，拳心朝后。目视前方。此为左丁步。右丁步动作与左丁步相同，唯有方向左右相反。（如图3-3-1所示）

动作要点：

上体正直，两腿紧靠。

四、弓步斜行

预备姿势：

两脚并步站立，两拳抱于腰间，拳心向上。目视前方。

the right shoulder, with the fist heart facing backward. Lower the left fist down to above the outer ankle bone of the left foot, with the fist heart facing backward. Gaze straight ahead. This stance is called the left T-stance. The right T-stance is performed in the same manner as the left T-stance, except the directions are reversed. (As shown in Fig. 3-3-1)

Key Points:

Keep the upper body straight and the legs close together.

图3-3-1
Fig.3-3-1

Ⅳ. Diagonal Bow Stance

Preparatory Posture:

Stand with the feet together, with two fists positioned at the waist with the fist hearts facing upward. Gaze straight ahead.

Movement Description:

Step to the left with the left foot. Turn the upper body 90 degrees to the left into a left bow stance. Extend the fists, with the right fist punching forward to the right and the left fist punching backward to the left. The right fist should stop above the left foot, and the left fist should stop behind the body. With the fist backs facing upward and the fist eyes aligned with each other, keep both arms level with the shoulders. Gaze toward the back-left. This exercise can be performed alternately on the left and right sides or while advancing. The actions are the same, except the directions are reversed. (As shown in Fig. 3-4-1)

动作说明：

左脚向左跨步，上体左转90度成左弓步，两拳分别向右前，向左后撑击，右拳停于左脚上方，左拳停于左后方。两拳拳背朝上，拳眼相对，双臂与肩平。目视左后方。此练习可左右交替或在行进间进行，动作相同，唯有方向相反。（如图3-4-1所示）

动作要点：

蹬地、拧腰、抖肩发力，两拳拳眼前后相对，力达两前臂外侧或拳外沿。

图3-4-1

Fig.3-4-1

图3-4-1

Fig.3-4-1

五、马步单鞭

预备姿势：

两脚并步站立，两拳抱于腰间，拳心向上。目视前方。

动作说明：

左脚向左跨一步，双脚平行，双膝外展，双腿屈膝下蹲成马步。同时，双臂屈肘经胸前向身体左右两侧撑击，双臂与肩平，力达双拳。目视左方。此动作可在原地或行进间左右进行练习，动作相同，唯有方向

Key Points:

Push off the ground, twist the waist, and shake the shoulders to generate force. Position the fists with fist eyes facing each other, one in front and one behind. Direct force to the outer sides of both forearms or the outer edges of both fists.

V. Horse Stance with Single Whip

Preparatory Posture:

Stand with the feet together, the fists positioned at the waist and the fist hearts facing upward. Gaze straight ahead.

Movement Description:

Step to the left with the left foot and keep the feet parallel. Extend the knees outward and squat down into a horse stance. At the same time, bend the arms at the elbows and push out to the left and right sides of the body from the front of the chest, keeping the arms level with the shoulders and directing the force through to the fists. Gaze toward the left. This movement can be practiced in place or while moving forward. The actions are the same, except the directions are reversed. (As shown in Fig. 3-5-1)

Key Points:

Keep the waist straight. Bend the arms and hold them close to the chest. When punching, shake the shoulders to generate power. Ensure the arms are level so as to direct the force through to the fists.

VI. Empty Stance with Uplift Palm

Preparatory Posture:

Stand with the feet together, the fists held at the waist, and the fist hearts facing upward. Gaze straight ahead.

Movement Description:

Step forward with the left foot and bend both knees until the right leg is parallel to the ground. Touch the ground lightly with the tip of the left foot, placing the body weight on the right leg to form a left empty stance. Meanwhile,

相反。（如图3-5-1所示）

动作要点：

腰要直，两臂屈抱要贴胸，冲拳时要抖肩发力，两臂平行，力达拳面。

图3-5-1
Fig.3-5-1

图3-5-1
Fig.3-5-1

六、虚步挑掌

预备姿势：

两脚并步站立，两拳抱于腰间，拳心向上。目视前方。

动作说明：

左脚向前，双腿屈膝下蹲至右腿与地面平行，左脚尖虚点地面，身体重心落在右腿成左虚步。同时，双拳变掌向上挑起，双臂交叉，右臂在前，左臂在后。目视前方。此动作可左右交替练习，动作相同，唯有方向相反。（如图3-6-1所示）

动作要点：

做虚步时要虚实分明，两腿紧靠、护裆。

open the fists into palms, lift them upward, and cross the arms, with the right arm positioned in front and the left arm behind. Gaze straight ahead. This movement can be practiced alternately on both sides, except the directions are reversed. (As shown in Fig. 3-6-1)

Key Points:

When performing the empty stance, ensure a clear distinction between the substantial and empty stances. Keep both legs close together, protecting the groin area.

图3-6-1
Fig.3-6-1

图3-6-1
Fig.3-6-1

Ⅶ. Flat Stance with Slicing Palm

Preparatory Posture:

Stand with the feet together. Position the fists at the waist with the fist hearts facing upward. Gaze straight ahead. (As shown in Fig. 3-7-1)

Movement Description:

Step to the right with the right foot, shift the body weight down onto the right leg, and bend the right knee into a full squat while keeping the left leg straight in a left flat stance. Keep the right fist in place, while opening the left fist into a palm and slicing downward from the waist along the inside of the left leg to about 5 cm above the left foot. Keep the palm facing downward, and the fingers pointing forward, and gaze toward the left. This movement can be

七、仆步切掌

预备姿势：

两脚并步站立，两拳抱于腰间，拳心向上。目视前方。（如图3-7-1所示）

动作说明：

右脚向右跨一步，身体重心下移至右腿，右腿屈膝全蹲，左腿绷直成左仆步。右拳不动，左拳变掌由腰部沿左腿内侧左下切至左脚面上侧约5厘米处。掌心朝下，掌指朝前。目视左方。此动作可左右交替练习，动作相同，唯有方向相反。（如图3-7-2所示）

动作要点：下蹲要迅速，拧腰、抖肩发力，力达掌外沿。

图3-7-1
Fig.3-7-1

图3-7-2
Fig.3-7-2

八、歇步冲拳

预备姿势：

两脚并步站立，两拳抱于腰间，拳心向上。目视前方。（如图

practiced alternately on both sides. The actions are the same except the directions are reversed. (As shown in Fig. 3-7-2)

Key Points:

Squat down quickly, twist the waist, and shake the shoulders to generate power, directing the force to the outer edge of the palm.

Ⅷ. Rest Stance with Punch Fist

Preparatory Posture:

Stand with the feet together, both fists positioned at the waist and the fist hearts facing upward. Gaze straight ahead. (As shown in Fig. 3-8-1)

Movement Description:

Step over with the right foot in front of the left leg toward the left side of the body, cross the legs, and bend the knees into a full squat to form a right rest stance. Meanwhile, keep the right fist in place, while striking forward with the left fist from the waist. Keep the surface of the fist facing right, the back of the fist facing upward, and the elbow bent. Gaze straight ahead. This action can be practiced alternately with both legs. The actions are the same except the directions are reversed. (As shown in Fig. 3-8-2)

Key Points:

Coordinate the upper and lower body movements. Ensure the rest stance is stable.

Ⅸ. Turning Body with Pushing Palm

Preparatory Posture:

Stand with the feet together, both fists positioned at the waist and the fist hearts facing upward. Gaze straight ahead. (As shown in Fig. 3-9-1)

Movement Description:

Step to the left with the left foot into a left bow stance, and turn the upper body 90 degrees to the left. Meanwhile, turn the left fist into a hooking hand. Move it upward across the chest to the right, and then downward across the abdomen to the left rear side, with the hook tip pointing upward and the arm

3-8-1所示）

动作说明：

右脚经左腿前方向身体左侧盖步，双腿交叉后屈膝全蹲成右歇步。同时，右拳不动，左拳由腰间向前方裹击，拳面朝右，拳背朝上，屈肘。目视前方。此动作可左右腿交替练习，动作相同，唯有方向相反。（如图3-8-2所示）

动作要点：

上下要协调，歇步要稳固。

图3-8-1
Fig. 3-8-1

图3-8-2
Fig.3-8-2

九、转身推掌

预备姿势：

两脚并步站立，两拳抱于腰间，拳心向上。目视前方。（如图3-9-1所示）

动作说明：

straight but close to the body. At the same time, turn the right fist into a palm and push it forward. Gaze straight ahead. The same action can be practiced in place by turning left and right alternately. The actions are the same except the directions are reversed. (As shown in Fig. 3-9-2)

Key Points:

Turn the body quickly. When pushing the palm, push off with the legs, twist the waist, and shake the shoulders so as to generate explosive power. Keep both arms slightly bent.

图3-9-1

Fig. 3-9-1

图3-9-2

Fig.3-9-2

左脚向左上步成左弓步，上体左转90度。同时，左拳变勾手，向上经胸前向右、向下经腹前搂至左后侧，勾尖向上，直臂贴身。同时，右拳变掌向前推掌。目视前方。此练习可原地左右转身交替进行，动作相同，唯有方向相反。（如图3-9-2所示）

动作要点：

左右转体动作要快，推掌要蹬腿、转腰、抖肩，迅猛发力，两臂保持微屈。

第四章

少林拳套路

Chapter 4

Shaolin Quan Routines

少林武术内容丰富，特点明显，体系完整。既有拳术、器械、对练，又有实战散打、技击功法等内容。其中少林拳又被誉为中国武坛四大名拳之一，而少林罗汉十八手、连环拳便是少林拳的优秀代表。

一、少林罗汉十八手

1. 动作名称

（1）预备势

（2）父子拱手

（3）怀中抱月

（4）白虎洗脸

（5）泥里拔葱

（6）上步推倒墙

（7）上步掠手

（8）扳掌

（9）右崩肘

（10）左崩肘

（11）揭手砍掌

（12）仙人摘茄

（13）猛虎转身

（14）破心肘

（15）转身崩肘

（16）转身金绞剪

（17）小猴抢瓜

（18）仙人归洞

（19）老虎靠山

（20）收势

Shaolin martial arts are rich in content, distinctive in characteristics, and complete in system. They include barehanded techniques, weapon forms, and sparring drills, as well as practical fighting and combat skills training. Among these, Shaolin quan is renowned as one of the four famous quan-styles in Chinese martial arts. Shaolin Arhat Eighteen Hands (*Luohan Shiba Shou*) and Interlinked Fist (*Lianhuan Quan*) are outstanding representatives of Shaolin quan.

Ⅰ. Arhat Eighteen Hands

1. Names of Movements

(1) Preparatory Posture

(2) Father and Son Fist Salutation

(3) Embrace the Moon

(4) White Tiger Washes Its Face

(5) Pluck Scallions from the Mud

(6) Step Forward to Push Down the Wall

(7) Step Forward to Rob the Hand

(8) Wrenching Palm

(9) Right Crack Elbow

(10) Left Crack Elbow

(11) Lift Hand and Chop with Palm

(12) Immortal Picks the Eggplant

(13) Ferocious Tiger Turns Around

(14) Heart-breaking Elbow

(15) Smash Elbow with Body Turn

(16) Golden Shear with Body Turn

(17) Little Monkey Steals the Melon

(18) Immortal Returns to the Cave

(19) Tiger Leans Against the Mountain

(20) Closing Form

2. Illustration of Movements

(1) Preparatory Posture

2. 动作图解

（1）预备势

动作说明：

身体直立，两脚并拢，两拳抱于腰间；目视前方。（如图4-1-1所示）

动作要点：

头正颈直，下颚微收，挺胸塌腰、收腹、夹腿。

图4-1-1

Fig.4-1-1

（2）父子拱手

动作说明：

左脚上前半步，右脚跟上成并步；两手由两侧向前屈肘交叉于胸前（插花手），右手在上，两掌心向外，掌指向上；目视两手。（如图4-1-2所示）

动作要点：

上步并步要迅速，两手要协调配合。

（3）怀中抱月（反掌）

动作说明：

Movement Description:

Stand upright with the feet together and both fists held at the waist. Gaze straight ahead. (As shown in Fig. 4-1-1)

Key Points:

Keep the head upright and the neck straight, with the chin slightly tucked. Straighten the chest, relax the lower back, draw in the abdomen, and keep the legs together.

(2) Father and Son Fist Salutation

Movement Description:

Step forward halfway with the left foot, and bring up the right foot to meet it. Move the hands from body sides to the front and cross them in front of the chest (called flower arranging hands), with the elbows bent, the right hand on top, the palms facing outward, and the fingers pointing upward. Gaze at the hands. (As shown in Fig. 4-1-2)

Key Points:

Step forward and bring the feet together swiftly, with both hands coordinated in action.

图4-1-2

Fig.4-1-2

(3) Embrace the Moon

Movement Description:

Keep the feet in place, sweep both hands simultaneously to the sides, then

两脚不动；两手同时向两侧拨，然后屈肘向胸前回掠，于胸前交叉成插手，左手在上，右手在下；目视两掌。（如图4-1-3所示）

动作要点：

双手插手，力达指间。

图4-1-3

Fig.4-1-3

（4）**白虎洗脸**

动作说明：

两脚不动；左手与右手环弧擦掌，右手向前向上屈肘推掌，掌指向上；目视前方。（如图4-1-4所示）

动作要点：

屈肘推掌有力，力达掌根。

（5）**泥里拔葱**

动作说明：

右脚不动，左脚跟离地提起，脚尖点地为虚步；左掌由上向右下方劈，右掌向右搂手后向左屈肘护胸，掌心向里；顺势两腿向下微蹲；上体左转45度；目视左方。（如图4-1-5所示）

动作要点：

劈掌拧腰抖肩，发力迅猛，动作连贯协调一致。

bend the elbows and draw the hands back toward the chest. Cross the hands in front of the chest with the left hand on top and the right one below. Gaze at the palms. (As shown in Fig. 4-1-3)

Key Points:

Cross the hands, with force delivered to the fingertips.

(4) White Tiger Washes Its Face

Movement Description:

Keep the feet in place. Move the left hand and right hand in an arc and rub the palms. Push the right palm forward and upward, with the elbow bent, the fingers pointing upward. Gaze straight ahead. (As shown in Fig. 4-1-4)

Key Points:

Bend the elbow to push the palm forcefully, delivering the force to the base of the palm.

图4-1-4

Fig.4-1-4

(5) Pluck Scallions from the Mud

Movement Description:

Keep the right foot in place. Touch the ground lightly with the tip of the left foot, forming an empty stance. Chop downward to the lower right with the left palm. Move the right palm to the right and bend the elbow to protect the chest, with the palm facing inward. Then, squat down slightly and turn the upper body 45 degrees to the left. Gaze at the left. (As shown in Fig. 4-1-5)

图4-1-5
Fig. 4-1-5

（6）**上步推倒墙**

动作说明：

左脚跟落地，上身向左转45度，右脚向前上一步，左腿蹬直成右弓步；两掌由下向前屈肘推出，两掌心向前，掌指向上；目视两掌。（如图4-1-6所示）

动作要点：

弓腿时膝与脚背垂直，后腿扣脚蹬直，松腰转髋，力达双掌。

（7）**上步掠手**

动作说明：

右脚不动，左脚上前一步，落于右脚外侧为虚步；同时上体右转90度；左掌回胸前由上向下向左劈，右手由右向左屈肘抢出，掌心向里护胸；目视左掌。（图4-1-7）

动作要点：

转身上步与劈掌同时进行，力达掌外侧。

Key Points:

Chop with the palm while twisting the waist and shaking the shoulders. Exert force swiftly and powerfully. Ensure the movements are fluid and coordinated.

(6) Step Forward to Push Down the Wall

Movement Description:

Lower the left heel to the ground, turn the upper body 45 degrees to the left, step forward with the right foot, and straighten the left leg to form a right bow stance. Thrust both palms forward from below with the elbows bent, the palms facing forward and the fingers pointing upward. Gaze at the palms. (As shown in Fig. 4-1-6)

Key Points:

When in the bow stance, keep the knee perpendicular to the instep, the back leg straight, and the foot turned inward. Relax the waist and rotate the hips, directing the force to both palms.

图4-1-6

Fig.4-1-6

(7) Step Forward to Rob the Hand

Movement Description:

Keep the right foot in place, step forward with the left foot, and place it outside the right foot to form an empty stance. Meanwhile, turn the upper body 90 degrees to the right; bring the left palm back to the front of the chest and chop downward to the left, while thrusting out the right hand from right to left, with the palm facing inward to protect the chest. Gaze at the left palm. (As shown in

图4-1-7

Fig.4-1-7

（8）**扳掌**

动作说明：

左脚跟落地，右脚不动，左脚向左横跨一步，使两腿成马步；左掌心由下向上向左侧屈肘扳掌，掌心向里，掌指向上，右掌置于腹前；目视左掌。（如图4-1-8所示）

动作要点：

上步变马步要迅速，扳掌有力。

（9）**右崩肘**

动作说明：

左脚碾地，右脚向前上一步，两脚碾地，体左转90度，成左弓步；右掌向前向外砍掌，然后屈肘向前，由右向左摆；目视右前方。（如图4-1-9所示）

动作要点：

松腰转髋，蹬腿发力，力达右肘。

Fig. 4-1-7)

Key Points:

Turn around, step forward, and chop with the palm at the same time, directing the force to the outer edge of the palm.

(8) Wrenching Palm

Movement Description:

Lower the left heel to the ground, keep the right foot in place, and step to the left with the left foot, forming a horse stance. Bend the left elbow and wrench the left palm upward to the left side, with the left palm facing inward and the fingers pointing upward, and the right palm staying in front of the abdomen. Gaze at the left palm. (As shown in Fig. 4-1-8)

Key Points:

Transition into the horse stance swiftly and wrench the palm forcefully.

图4-1-8

Fig.4-1-8

(9) Right Crack Elbow

Movement Description:

Pivot on the left foot and step forward with the right foot. Next, pivot on both feet and turn the body 90 degrees to the left, forming a left bow stance. Chop forward and outward with the right palm. Bend the elbow and sweep it forward from right to left. Gaze toward the front right. (As shown in Fig. 4-1-9)

Key Points:

Relax the waist, rotate the hips, and push off with the leg to generate power,

图4-1-9
Fig.4-1-9

（10）**左崩肘**

动作说明：

两脚碾地，上体右转180度，左脚向前跨一步，屈膝，两腿成左弓步；左掌向右前方领起，然后起肘上崩、前顶，右掌收于腰间；目视前方。（如图4-1-10所示）

动作要点：

转身退步，力达左肘。

（11）**揭手砍掌**

动作说明：

右脚不动，收左脚落于右脚内侧成虚步；顺势上身右转，两腿屈膝下蹲；左掌由上向左下方砍，右掌护胸；目视左侧。（如图4-1-11所示）

动作要点：

下蹲砍掌，协调有力。

directing the force to the right elbow.

(10) Left Crack Elbow

Movement Description:

Pivot on both feet, turn the upper body 180 degrees to the right, step forward with the left foot, and bend the knee, forming a left bow stance. Lead with the left palm to the front right, then raise the elbow and thrust it upward and forward, with the right palm held at the waist. Gaze straight ahead. (As shown in Fig. 4-1-10)

Key Points:

Turn around and step back, directing the force to the left elbow.

图4-1-10
Fig.4-1-10

(11) Lift Hand and Chop with Palm

Movement Description:

Keep the right foot in place and place the left foot next to the inside of the right foot, forming an empty stance. Then, turn the upper body to the right, squat down, chop downward to the lower left with the left palm, and guard the chest with the right palm. Gaze on the left side. (As shown in Fig. 4-1-11)

Key Points:

The squatting and the chopping should be coordinated and forceful.

(12) Immortal Picks the Eggplant

Movement Description:

Step forward with the right foot, lift the right knee, and turn the upper body

图4-1-11
Fig.4-1-11

（12）仙人摘茄

动作说明：

右脚向前上一步，右腿提膝，上身右转45度；左掌向左撩掌，右手向前向下猛抢，掌心向上，掌指向前；目视右掌。（如图4-1-12所示）

动作要点：

提膝脚面绷直，抢手短促有力，以腰催肩，以肩带劲，插掌后自然弹回。

（13）猛虎转身

动作说明：

右脚向前侧落一步，两脚碾地，体左转180度成左弓步；同时两手向前抓，然后两掌回胸前，屈肘插掌；目视前方。（如图4-1-13所示）

动作要点：

转身落弓步要迅速，插掌有力。

to the right by 45 degrees. Sweep the left palm to the left. Thrust the right hand forward and downward, with the palm facing upward and the fingers pointing forward. Gaze at the right palm. (As shown in Fig. 4-1-12)

Key Points:

Lift the knee with the instep stretched straight. Thrust the hand quickly and forcefully, using the waist to drive the shoulder and the shoulder to guide the force. After thrusting the palm, snap it back naturally.

图4-1-12

Fig. 4-1-12

(13) Ferocious Tiger Turns Around

Movement Description:

Step forward and to the side with the right foot, pivot on both feet, and turn the body 180 degrees to the left, forming a left bow stance. Meanwhile, reach forward with both hands to grab, and then bring both palms back in front of the chest. Next, bend the elbows and thrust the palms forward. Gaze straight ahead. (As shown in Fig. 4-1-13)

Key Points:

Turn and transition into the bow stance quickly. Thrust the palms forcefully.

(14) Heart-breaking Elbow

Movement Description:

Pivot on both feet, turn the body 180 degrees to the right, and step forward with the right foot, forming a right bow stance. Lift the right elbow and swing

图4-1-13
Fig.4-1-13

（14）破心肘

动作说明：

两脚碾地，体右转180度，右脚向前上一步，成右弓步；右拳起肘向前向右摆，拳心向下，左拳向右落砸击右臂，顺势再向右击右肘端（响亮）；目视前方。（如图4-1-14所示）

动作要点：

松腰转髋，蹬腿发力，力达右肘。

（15）转身崩肘

动作说明：

左脚向前上一步，两脚碾地，体右转90度成马步；两手随势架肘，同时向两侧崩击；目视前方。（如图4-1-15所示）

动作要点：

转身迅速，双肘同时发力。

the right fist forward and to the right, with the fist heart facing downward. Hit with the left fist, the right arm and then the right elbow with force (producing a sound). Gaze straight ahead. (As shown in Fig. 4-1-14)

Key Points:

Relax the waist, rotate the hips, push off with the leg to generate power, directing the force to the right elbow.

图4-1-14

Fig.4-1-14

(15)) Smash Elbow with Body Turn

Movement Description:

Step forward with the left foot, pivot on both feet, and turn the body 90 degrees to the right, forming a horse stance. Meanwhile, raise the elbows and smash the elbows outward to both sides. Gaze straight ahead. (As shown in Fig. 4-1-15)

Key Points:

Turn around quickly and smash both elbows forcefully at the same time.

(16) Golden Shear with Body Turn

Movement Description:

Pivot on both feet and turn the body 90 degrees to the right. Step forward with the left foot, and bend the left knee, forming a left bow stance. Simultaneously bring both palms back and cross them in front of the chest, with the elbows bent, the left hand being outside, the right hand being inside, and the

图4-1-15
Fig.4-1-15

（16）转身金绞剪势

动作说明：

两脚碾地体右转90度，左脚向前上一步，左腿屈膝成左弓步；同时两掌回胸前屈肘交叉，左手在外、右手在内，两掌心向外；目视两手。（如图4-1-16所示）

动作要点：

转身上步变弓步，屈肘插手。

（17）小猴抢瓜

动作说明：

右脚向前上一步，两脚碾地，体左转90度两腿成马步，顺势上体左转45度，两掌由右向左前方抓，然后屈肘内搂，掌心向里；目视右侧。（如图4-1-17所示）

动作要点：

马步中心落两腿之间，撩爪迅速。

palms facing outward. Gaze at the hands. (As shown in Fig. 4-1-16)

Key Points:

Turn the body and step forward into the bow stance with the hands crossed and the elbows bent.

图4-1-16

Fig.4-1-16

(17) Little Monkey Steals the Melon

Movement Description:

Step forward with the right foot, pivot on both feet, and turn the body 90 degrees to the left, forming a horse stance. Simultaneously, turn the upper body 45 degrees to the left, reach forward from right to left with both palms to grab, then bend the elbows and sweep inward, with the palms facing inward. Gaze toward the right. (As shown in Fig. 4-1-17)

Key Points:

In the horse stance, center the weight between the two legs, and swipe quickly with the claw.

(18) Immortal Returns to the Cave

Movement Description:

Bring the left foot to meet the right foot, standing with both feet together. Sweep both palms from the inside to the outside. Bring them back to the front of the chest. Bend the elbows upward into an interlocking position with the fingers pointing upward and the palms facing outward. Gaze straight ahead. (As shown in Fig. 4-1-18)

图4-1-17

Fig.4-1-17

（18）**仙人归洞**

动作说明：

收左脚与右脚成并步；两掌由内向外撩打，然后回胸前向上屈肘成插手，掌指向上，掌心向外；目视前方。（如图4-1-18所示）

动作要点：

并步直立，挺胸抬头。

（19）**老虎靠山**

动作说明：

右脚向左横跨一步，屈膝成左弓步；两手同时由下向上推出，然后变拳向前冲击，右拳屈肘护胸，左拳屈肘护腰；目视右侧。（如图4-1-19所示）

动作要点：

弓腿时膝与脚背垂直，大腿保持水平，力达肘尖。

Key Points:

Stand upright with the feet put together, the chest puffed out, and the head kept up.

图4-1-18

Fig.4-1-18

(19) Tiger Leans Against the Mountain

Movement Description:

Step to the left with the right foot and bend the knees, forming a left bow stance. Simultaneously push both hands upward from below, then change them into fists and thrust them forward. Bend the right elbow to protect the chest and the left elbow to protect the waist. Gaze to the right. (As shown in Fig. 4-1-19)

Key Points:

When in a bow stance, keep the knee perpendicular to the instep and the thigh horizontal. Direct the force to the tip of the elbow.

(20) Closing Form

Movement Description:

Bring the left foot to meet the right foot, standing with feet together. Keep fingers of both hands together. Move the hands in an arc in front of the chest. Place the hands by the sides of the thighs with the palms facing inward, the chest out, and the back straight. Gaze straight ahead. (As shown in Fig. 4-1-20)

Key Points:

Bring the feet together and draw the hands back simultaneously in a

图4-1-19
Fig.4-1-19

（20）收势

动作说明：

收左脚与右脚并步站立；两手五指并拢，在胸前环弧后下垂，贴于大腿两侧下方，掌心向里，身胸挺直；目视前方。（如图4-1-20所示）

动作要点：

并步与收掌同时进行，协调一致，挺胸收腹。

二、连环拳

1. 动作名称

（1）预备势

（2）起势

（3）左格冲心拳

（4）十字蹬腿

（5）马步冲拳

（6）击手炮

coordinated and consistent manner, with the chest puffed out and abdomen tucked in.

图4-1-20

Fig.4-1-20

Ⅱ. Interlinked Fist

1. Names of Movement

(1) Preparatory Posture

(2) Commencing Form

(3) Left Block and Heart Striking Punch

(4) Snap Kick in Cross Stance

(5) Straight Punch in Horse Stance

(6) Strike Palm and Stomp Foot

(7) Overhead Block and Straight Punch in Horse Stance

(8) Right Push Palm in Bow Stance

(9) Left Push Palm in Bow Stance

(10) Hook Hand in Flat Stance

(11) Push Palm in Bow Stance

(12) Clap Foot in Cross Stance

(13) Overhead Push Palm in Bow Stance

（7）上架马步冲拳

（8）弓步右推掌

（9）弓步左推掌

（10）仆步勾手

（11）弓步推掌

（12）十字拍脚

（13）弓步架推掌

（14）金鸡独立

（15）上步探花

（16）双开门

（17）弓步双冲拳

（18）击手拍脚

（19）弓步顶肘

（20）转身下插掌

（21）虚步架冲拳

（22）英雄坐山

（23）收势

2. 动作图解

（1）预备势

动作说明：

两脚并步而立，双手自然下垂贴于体侧，头正身直，两眼平视前方。（如图4-2-1所示）

动作要点：

头正颈直，挺胸、收腹、立腰、直背，眼神有力。

(14) Golden Rooster Stands on One Leg

(15) Step Forward and Seek Flower

(16) Double Opening

(17) Straight Punches in Bow Stance

(18) Strike Hand and Slap Foot

(19) Elbow Strike in Bow Stance

(20) Turn Around and Thrust Palm Downward

(21) Overhead Block and Straight Punch in Empty Stance

(22) Hero Sits on the Mountain

(23) Closing Form

2. Illustration of Movement

(1) Preparatory Posture

Movement Description:

Stand with the feet together, with the hands naturally hanging down at the sides of the body. Keep the head straight and the body upright, with the eyes gazing straight ahead. (As shown in Fig. 4-2-1)

Key Points:

Keep the head straight and the neck aligned, the chest out, the abdomen in, the waist firm, the back straight, and the gaze focused.

(2) Commencing Form

Movement Description:

Clench both hands into fists and strike the elbow backward, with the fist hearts facing upward and the fists positioned next to the waist. Turn the head to the left. Keep the chest out, the abdomen tucked in, and the tongue pressing against the upper palate. Gaze to the left. (As shown in Fig. 4-2-2)

Key Points:

Keep the chest out, the abdomen in, and the waist straight. Tuck the elbows in tightly, while keeping the fists no higher than your abdomen. When turning your head, your gaze should be strong and focused.

图4-2-1
Fig.4-2-1

（2）**起势**

动作说明：

两手变拳，拳心朝上向后撞肘，抱于腰间，头向左摆，挺胸收腹，舌抵上腭。目视左方。（如图4-2-2所示）

动作要点：

挺胸、收腹、立腰，肘部要向内夹紧，拳面不过腹部，摆头时眼神有力。

（3）**左格冲心拳**

动作说明：

身体左转90度，左脚向前上步成左弓步。左小臂左上格出，收于腰间，拳心朝上。同时，右拳向前冲出，力达拳面，拳心朝下，臂与肩平。目视前方。（如图4-2-3所示）

动作要点：

左转、左脚上步与左小臂左上格挡三动作同时完成，上动不停，蹬腿、转腰、顺肩，力达右拳。

图4-2-2
Fig.4-2-2

(3) Left Block and Heart Striking Punch

Movement Description:

Turn the body 90 degrees to the left. Step forward with the left foot, forming a left bow stance. Raise the left forearm upward to the left, and then retract it back to the waist, with the fist heart facing upward. Meanwhile, thrust the right fist forward with the force concentrated on the fist face, the fist heart facing downward, and the arm level with the shoulder. Gaze straight ahead. (As shown in Fig. 4-2-3)

Key Points:

Turn left, step forward with the left foot, and block with the left forearm simultaneously. Without pausing, push off with the legs, rotate the waist, and follow through with the shoulder, directing the force to the right fist.

(4) Snap Kick in a Cross Stance

Movement Description:

Following the previous movement, lift the right foot and snap it forward and upward. Meanwhile, retract the right fist back to the waist with the fist heart facing upward. Thrust the left fist forward with the fist heart facing downward. Keep the arm level with the shoulder, and direct the force through to the left fist. Gaze straight ahead. (As shown in Fig. 4-2-4)

图4-2-3
Fig.4-2-3

（4）十字蹬腿

动作说明：

接上动，右脚提起上勾向前弹蹬，同时右拳拳心朝上收回腰间。左拳拳心朝下向前冲出，臂与肩平，力达左拳。目视前方。（如图4-2-4所示）

动作要点：

右脚前蹬、左拳前冲、右拳收回三动作同时完成，左支撑腿稳固。

Key Points:

Kick with the right foot, thrust out the left fist, and draw back the right fist simultaneously. Keep the left supporting leg stable.

图4-2-4

Fig.4-2-4

(5) Straight Punch in Horse Stance

Movement Description:

Turn the body 90 degrees to the left, step to the right with the right foot, forming a horse stance with feet parallel, knees pointing outward, and both legs bent. Meanwhile, retract the left fist to the waist with the fist heart facing upward, and punch with the right fist to the right and the fist heart facing downward. Keep the arm level with the shoulder, and direct force through to the right fist. Turn the head to the right and gaze to the right. (As shown in Fig. 4-2-5)

Key Points:

Lower the right foot on the ground, pull the left fist back, and thrust the right fist out simultaneously. Keep the head straight, the neck upright, the waist firm, and the back straight. Maintain a stable horse stance with full spirit and energy.

（5）马步冲拳

动作说明：

身体左转90度，右脚向右落地成马步，双脚平行，双膝外展，双腿下蹲。同时，左拳拳心朝上收回腰间，右拳拳心朝下向右冲出，臂与肩平，力达右拳。向右摆头，目视右方。（如图4-2-5所示）

动作要点：

右脚落地、左拳收回、右拳冲出三动作同时完成，头正颈直，立腰直背，马步稳固，精神充足。

图4-2-5

Fig.4-2-5

（6）击手炮

动作说明：

左脚不动，右脚提起与左脚相并震地，双腿下蹲。左拳变掌前下移，右拳拳面向左下与左掌掌心相击于膝前。目视前方。（如图4-2-6所示）

动作要点：

震脚、击掌同时完成，头正颈直，立腰直背。

(6) Strike Palm and Stomp Foot

Movement Description:

Keep the left foot in place, lift the right foot, bring it together with the left foot, and then stomp down. Squat down with both legs. Turn the left fist into a palm and moves it downward in front, and strikes the left palm with the face of the right fist in front of the knees. Gaze straight ahead. (As shown in Figure 4-2-6)

Key Points:

Stomp the feet and strike the palm simultaneously. Keep the head straight and the neck upright, with an erect waist and a straight back.

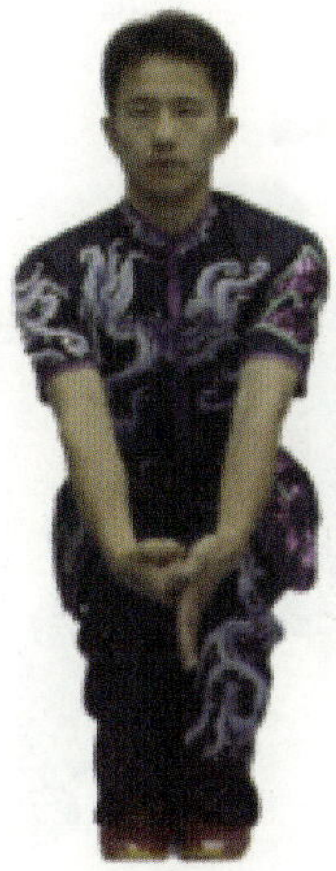

图4-2-6

Fig.4-2-6

(7) Overhead Block and Straight Punch in Horse Stance

Movement Description:

Turn the body 180 degrees to the right, and jump into a horse stance with feet parallel and knees spread outward. Simultaneously, move the right fist upward past the chest to about 8 centimeters above the head, with the fist heart facing downward. Retract the left fist from in front of the knee back to the waist, and then thrust it out to the left with the fist heart facing downward, directing force to the left fist. Gaze to the left. (As shown in Fig. 4-2-7)

（7）上架马步冲拳

动作说明：

身体右后转180度，双脚跳步成马步，双脚平行，双膝外展。同时，右拳经胸前向上架于头顶上方约8厘米处，拳心朝下，左拳从膝前收至腰间，拳心朝下向左冲出，力达左拳。目视左方。（如图4-2-7所示）

动作要点：

转身落地马步、右拳架于头顶、左拳冲出三动作同时完成，转身跳步落地稳固，头正颈直，立腰直背，眼神有力。

图4-2-7
Fig.4-2-7

（8）弓步右推掌

动作说明：

身体左转90度，右腿向前上步成右弓步。同时，右拳变立掌下落于左胸前，左拳变掌向右上经右肩和右臂外侧向下收于腰间，掌心朝上，右掌变立掌向前推出，力达右掌。目视前方。（如图4-2-8所示）

动作要点：

滚身上右步，手脚协调运作，气力顺达。

Key Points:

Turn into the horse stance, raise the right fist above the head, and thrust out the left fist simultaneously. Ensure a stable landing after the turning jump, keep the head straight, the neck upright, the waist erect, and the back straight. Maintain a focused gaze.

(8) Right Push Palm in Bow Stance

Movement Description:

Turn the body 90 degrees to the left, and step forward with the right leg, forming a right bow stance. Simultaneously, turn the right fist into a palm and lower it to the front of the left chest. Turn the left fist into a palm and move it upward to the right, passing the right shoulder and the outside of the right arm, then put it downward to the waist with the palm facing upward. Push the right palm forward with force. Gaze straight ahead. (As shown in Fig. 4-2-8)

Key Points:

Roll the body and step forward with the right foot. Coordinate the movements of both hands and feet, allowing the force to flow smoothly.

图4-2-8

Fig.4-2-8

(9) Left Push Palm in Bow Stance

Movement Description:

Following the previous movement, maintain the right bow stance. Retract the right palm, with the palm facing upward, back to the waist. Meanwhile, transform the left hand into a vertical palm and push it forward, with force directed through to the left palm. Gaze straight ahead. (As shown in Fig. 4-2-9)

Key Points:

Bring the right palm back and push the left palm out simultaneously in

（9）弓步左推掌

动作说明：

接上动，右弓步不变。右掌掌心朝上收于腰间，同时，左手变立掌向前推出，力达左掌。目视前方。（如图4-2-9所示）

动作要点：

右掌的收回与左掌的推出同时完成，协调一致，双腿配合发力。

图4-2-9

Fig.4-2-9

（10）仆步勾手

动作说明：

身体左转90度，右腿绷直下落，左腿屈膝全蹲成右仆步。同时左掌下落，经左膝前向后变勾手，指尖向上背于腰后部。右臂内旋下落，与左臂相应运行，经裆部向上，立掌放于左胸前。目视右方。（如图4-2-10所示）

动作要点：

转身成仆步迅速，两脚全脚掌着地，头正颈直，向右摆头挺胸、收腹、立腰、直背，眼睛有神。

coordination. Coordinate the efforts of both legs to generate force.

(10) Hook Hand in Flat Stance

Movement Description:

Turn the body 90 degrees to the left, straighten the right leg, and bend the left leg into a flat stance. Meanwhile, lower the left palm, move it past the front of the left knee, and transform it into a hook hand, with the fingertips pointing upward behind the waist. Rotate the right arm inward, and move it along with the left arm, passing through the groin area and then upward, placing the vertical palm in front of the left chest. Gaze to the right. (As shown in Fig. 4-2-10)

Key Points:

Turn the body into a flat stance swiftly, with both feet fully on the ground. Keep the head straight and neck upright. Turn the head to the right, with the chest out, the abdomen in, the waist upright, the back straight, and the gaze focused.

图4-2-10

Fig.4-2-10

(11) Pushing Palm with Bow Stance

Movement Description:

Shift the weight to the right when standing. Rotate the body 90 degrees to the right, and slightly draw the left leg forward into a right bow stance. Meanwhile, move the right palm toward the right from the left chest to the groin area, and to the right knee. Change the orientation of the palm and retract it to the waist. Turn the left hand into an upright palm and thrust it forward, directing force through to the left palm. Gaze straight ahead. (As shown in Fig. 4-2-11)

（11）弓步推掌

动作说明：

起身重心右移，身体右转90度，左腿微前收成右弓步。同时，右掌自左胸前经裆部向右，于右膝前变掌收于腰间。左手变立掌向前推出，力达左掌。目视前方。（如图4-2-11所示）

动作要点：

仆步起身、蹬腿、收腹、立腰、头正颈直、顺肩发力推掌。

图4-2-11
Fig.4-2-11

（12）十字拍脚

动作说明：

左掌掌心朝上收于腰间。提左膝，脚尖绷直，向前上方弹踢。同时，右手自腰间内旋变掌前伸以掌心击打左脚面。目视前方。（如图4-2-12所示）

动作要点：

左掌收回、左腿弹踢、右掌击打左脚面三动作同时完成。头正、颈直、收腹、立腰、直背、眼睛有神。

Key Points:

Rise from the flat stance. Keep the legs stressed, the abdomen tucked in, the waist erect, the head upright, and the neck straight. Use the force from the shoulder to push the palm.

(12) Clap Foot in Cross Stance

Movement Description:

Retract the left hand to the waist with the palm facing upward. Lift the left knee, straighten the toes, and snap kick forward and upward. Meanwhile, rotate the right hand inward from the waist, extend it forward, and strike the top of the left foot with the palm. Gaze straight ahead. (As shown in Fig. 4-2-12)

Key Points:

Retract the left palm, snap kick with the left leg, and strike the top of the left foot with the right palm simultaneously. Keep the head upright, the neck straight, the abdomen tucked in, the waist erected, the back straight, and the gaze focused.

图4-2-12

Fig.4-2-12

(13) Overhead Push Palm in Bow Stance

Movement Description:

Following the previous movement, step forward with the left leg into a left bow stance. Meanwhile, raise the right palm about 8 centimeters above the head, with the palm facing upward. Keep the left palm upright and push it forward, directing the force through to the left palm. Gaze straight ahead. (As shown in Fig. 4-2-13)

（13）弓步架推掌

动作说明：

上动不停，左腿向前落地成左弓步。同时，右掌向上架于头顶上方约8厘米处，掌心朝上，左掌变立掌向前推出，力达左掌。目视前方。（如图4-2-13所示）

动作要点：

落步、架掌、推掌三动作同时完成。动作协调一气，头正、颈直、收腹、立腰、直背，眼睛有神。

图4-2-13

Fig.4-2-13

（14）金鸡独立

动作说明：

身体右后转180度，右脚提起绷直放于左膝前上方。同时，左掌变拳拳心朝上放于右腹前，右肘下落，右前臂竖立向外格挡，掌心朝左，力达右臂。目视前方。（如图4-2-14所示）

动作要点：

转身、提膝、格挡三者一气呵成，支撑腿稳固有力。头正、颈直、收腹、立腰、直背，眼睛有神。

Key Points:

Turn into the bow stance, push the palm, and raise the palm simultaneously. Keep the movements coordinated and fluid, with the head upright, the neck straight, the abdomen in, the waist erected, the back straight, and the gaze focused.

(14) Golden Rooster Stands on One Leg

Movement Description:

Turn the body 180 degrees to the right, lift the right leg, and keep it straight, positioning it in front of and above the left knee. Meanwhile, turn the left palm into a fist with the fist heart facing upward, positioning it in front of the right abdomen. Lower the right elbow, raise the right forearm upward, and block outward with the palm facing left, directing force through the right arm. Gaze straight ahead. (As shown in Fig. 4-2-14)

Key Points:

Turn the body, lift the knee, and block seamlessly as one fluid motion, with the supporting leg stable and strong. Keep the head upright, the neck straight, the abdomen tucked in, the waist erect, the back straight, and the gaze focused.

图4-2-14

Fig.4-2-14

(15) Step Forward and Seek Flower

Movement Description:

Following the previous movement, turn the body 90 degrees to the right, place the right foot on the ground, and step forward with the left foot into a left bow stance. Meanwhile, move the left fist upward along the outside of the right

（15）**上步探花**

动作说明：

上动不停，身体右转90度，右脚落地，左脚向左上步成左弓步。同时，左拳经右臂外侧向上，置于左耳前上方，拳心朝下，力达左臂，右掌自左胸前变拳由左臂下侧向前冲出，力达右拳。目视前方。（如图4-2-15所示）

动作要点：

马步落稳，动作连贯，蹬腿转腰，顺肩发力。头正、颈直、收腹、立腰、直背，眼睛有神。

图4-2-15
Fig.4-2-15

（16）**双开门**

动作说明：

右脚提起绷直放于左膝前上方，同时，两肘下落，竖前臂于胸前，双手变掌，两臂内旋外格，掌心朝前，力达双臂。目视前方。（如图4-2-16所示）

动作要点：

右脚提膝、两臂内旋外格两者同时完成，支撑腿稳固有力。头正、颈直、收腹、立腰、直背，眼睛有神。

arm, positioning it in front of and above the left ear, with the fist heart facing downward, and the force directed through the left arm. Turn the right palm into a fist in front of the left chest and thrust it forward from below the left arm, with force directed through to the right fist. Gaze straight ahead. (As shown in Fig. 4-2-15)

Key Points:

Ensure the horse stance is stable and the movements are fluid. Push off with the legs, rotate the waist, and follow through with the shoulder to generate force. Keep the head straight, the neck upright, the abdomen tucked in, the waist firm, and the back straight. Maintain a focused and spirited gaze.

(16) Double Opening

Movement Description:

Lift the right foot, keep it straightened, and place it in front of and above the left knee. Meanwhile, lower both elbows, position the forearms upright in front of the chest, and turn both hands into palms. Rotate both arms inward and then outward to block, with the palms facing forward and the force directed through to both arms. Gaze straight ahead. (As shown in Fig. 4-2-16)

Key Points:

Lift the right foot and rotate arms inward and block outward simultaneously. Ensure the supporting leg is stable and strong. Keep the head upright, the neck straight, the abdomen in, the waist erect, the back straight, and the gaze focused.

图4-2-16

Fig.4-2-16

（17）弓步双冲拳

动作说明：

上动不停，右脚向前落地，两手握拳，拳心朝上，收于腰间。左脚向前上步成左弓步，双拳拳心朝下向前冲出，两臂与肩平，力达双拳。目视前方。（如图4-2-17所示）

动作要点：

蹬腿发力冲拳，头正、颈直、收腹、立腰、直背，眼睛有神。

图4-2-17
Fig.4-2-17

（18）击手拍脚

动作说明：

接上动，提右膝，脚尖绷直，向前上弹踢，双拳变掌，右掌用掌背击打左掌心，同时右掌心击打右脚面。目视前方。（如图4-2-18所示）

动作要点：

左掌、右掌、右脚面合成一击，支撑腿稳固有力。头正、颈直、收腹、立腰、直背，眼睛有神。

(17) Straight Punches in Bow Stance

Movement Description:

Following the previous movement, step forward with the right foot. Clench the hands into fists with the fist hearts facing upward. Put both fists to the waist. Step forward with the left foot, forming a left bow stance. Thrust both fists forward, with the fist hearts facing downward, the arms level with the shoulders, and the force reaching both fists. Gaze straight ahead. (As shown in Fig. 4-2-17)

Key Points:

Push off with the leg to generate force for the punch. Keep the head straight, the neck upright, the abdomen in, the waist erect, the back straight, and the gaze focused.

(18) Strike Hand and Slap Foot

Movement Description:

Following the previous movement, lift the right knee with the toes pointed straight. Perform a forward and upward snap kick, and turn both fists into palms. Use the back of the right palm to strike the center of the left palm while simultaneously striking the right instep with the right palm. Gaze straight ahead. (As shown in Fig. 4-2-18)

Key Points:

Strike simultaneously, with the supporting leg stable and strong. Keep the head straight, the neck upright, the abdomen tucked in, the waist firm, the back straight, and the gaze focused.

图4-2-18

Fig.4-2-18

（19）弓步顶肘

动作说明：

上动不停，右脚向前落地成右弓步。同时，双手回收于胸前，右手握拳抵于左手掌心，左掌推动右拳使右肘向前撞击，力达肘尖。目视前方。（如图4-2-19所示）

动作要点：

右脚落地、顶肘、目视前方三者同时完成。头正、颈直、收腹、立腰、直背，眼睛有神。

图4-2-19
Fig.4-2-19

（20）转身下插掌

动作说明：

身体左转180度成左弓步，右手变掌掌心朝前向左膝前下插出，力达右掌。左掌掌心朝下贴于右臂二头肌上，目视前方。（如图4-2-20所示）

动作要点：

蹬右腿、转身、下插掌三者同时完成。头正、颈直、收腹、立腰、直背，眼睛有神。

(19) Elbow Strike in Bow Stance

Movement Description:

Following the previous movement, step forward with the right foot into a right bow stance. Meanwhile, bring both hands back to the front of the chest, with the right hand clenched into a fist against the palm of the left hand. Push the right fist with the left palm and thrust the right elbow forward with the force delivered to the tip of the elbow. Gaze straight ahead. (As shown in Fig. 4-2-19)

Key Points:

Step down with the right foot, thrust out the elbow, and gaze straight ahead at the same time. Keep the head straight, the neck upright, the abdomen in, the waist upright, the back straight, and the gaze focused.

(20) Turn Around and Thrust Palm Downward

Movement Description:

Turn the body 180 degrees to the left into a left bow stance. Transform the right hand into a forward-facing palm, and thrust it downward in front of the left knee, with force delivered to the right palm. Rest the left palm facing downward on the right bicep. Gaze straight ahead. (As shown in Fig. 4-2-20)

Key Points:

Push off with the right leg, turn the body, and thrust the palm downward simultaneously. Keep the head upright, the neck straight, the abdomen in, the waist erect, the back straight, and the gaze focused.

图4-2-20

Fig.4-2-20

（21）虚步架冲拳

动作说明：

身体右转90度，重心移于右腿，左脚提起放于右脚前方，脚尖点地，右腿下蹲成左虚步。同时，右手握拳，拳心朝下架于头顶上方约8厘米处。左手握拳，拳心朝下向前冲出，臂与肩平，力达左拳，目视前方。（如图4-2-21所示）

动作要点：

左虚步、冲拳、架拳同时完成。头正、颈直、收腹、立腰、直背，眼睛有神。

图4-2-21

Fig.4-2-21

（22）英雄坐山

动作说明：

左脚向左跨步成马步，同时双手变拳自头顶向体侧划弧下砸。接上动不停，右脚提起向左脚内侧并步震脚，同时左脚离地，双手前臂十字交叉相合击于腹前。接上动不停，左脚向左跨步落成马步，同时右拳经胸前向上格挡架于头顶，拳心朝下，左拳左下格，停置于左膝上，拳背朝前，拳心朝后。目视左上方。（如图4-2-22所示）

(21) Overhead Block and Straight Punch in Empty Stance

Movement Description:

Turn the body 90 degrees to the right, shifting the weight to the right leg. Lift the left foot and place it in front of the right foot, with the toe touching the ground. Squat down on the right leg to form a left empty stance. Meanwhile, clench the right hand into a fist, with the palm facing downward, positioned about 8 centimeters above the head. Clench the left hand into a fist with the palm facing downward, and thrust it forward, with the arm level with the shoulder. Direct the force through to the left fist. Gaze straight ahead. (As shown in Fig. 4-2-21)

Key Points:

Transition into the left empty stance, thrust out the fist, and position the fist simultaneously. Keep the head straight, the neck upright, the abdomen in, the waist erect, the back straight, and the gaze focused.

(22) Hero Sits on Mountain

Movement Description:

Step to the left with the left foot to form a horse stance. Clench both hands into fists and swing them downward in an arc motion from above the head to the sides of the body. Without pausing, lift the right foot and put it next to the inside of the left foot. Stomp the foot, and at the same time, lift the left foot off the ground, and cross both forearms in front of the abdomen and strike them together. Without pausing, step to the left with the left foot, forming a horse stance. Simultaneously, move the right fist upward past the chest to block above the head with the fist heart facing downward. Move the left fist downward to block, stopping it above the left knee with the fist back facing forward and the fist heart facing backward. Gaze to the upper left. (As shown in Fig. 4-2-22)

Key Points:

Ensure that the horse stance is light yet stable. Stomp forcefully, making sure that the movements are coordinated and continuous. Keep the head straight, the neck upright, the abdomen in, the waist erect, the back straight, and the gaze focused.

(23) Closing Form

Movement Description:

Take the left foot back next to the right foot. Simultaneously, turn both fists

动作要点：

马步轻固、震脚有力、动作协调连贯。头正、颈直、收腹、立腰、直背，眼睛有神。

图4-2-22

Fig.4-2-22

（23）收势

动作说明：

左脚收回与右脚并步而立。同时，两拳变掌以左手背相击右掌心于头顶上方，向两侧分掌下落，双掌变拳，收于腰间。目视前方。（如图

into palms and strike the back of the left hand against the center of the right palm above the head. Separate the palms and lower them to the body sides, then turn the palms back into fists and retract them back to the waist. Gaze straight ahead. (As shown in Fig. 4-2-23)

Key Points:

Strike palms above the head, bring feet together, and retract the fists. Ensure the movement is smooth and coordinated. Keep the head upright, the neck straight, the abdomen in, the waist erect, the back straight, and the gaze focused.

图4-2-23

Fig.4-2-23

4-2-23所示）

动作要点：

头顶击掌，并步收拳，动作连贯协调。头正、颈直、收腹、立腰、直背，眼睛有神。

第五章

少林拳实战技法

Chapter 5

Shaolin Quan Combating Skills

少林拳的实战技法丰富多变。其特点是招招相连，随机应变，攻防莫测，视退而实进，奥妙无穷。失局时设伏诱敌，乘虚而入，虚则实，实则虚，虚虚实实，真真假假。利局时立意坚强，发力迅猛，出手决断。充分显示少林拳刚健有力、结构严谨、节奏分明、造诣高深的特点。在实战中，少林拳招法分远战法和近战法。远战时以拳、脚功夫为主；近距离打法则是靠身近战。靠身招法是以肩、胯结合膝、肘制胜。这些招法往往能形成一些可利用的、有利的机会，打乱对手阵脚，迫使对手无招架之力，及至将对手制服。

一、罗汉十八手实战技法

1. 弓步冲拳

动作说明：（穿黑色衣者为甲，穿白衣者为乙）

（1）乙方：右脚在前，左脚在后（或左脚在前，右脚在后），用右拳经右外侧向前摆动击打甲方左耳部。甲方：立即使左脚在前，右脚在后；左手从身前屈肘向上，经额前向左绕环，用前臂近腕处桡骨一侧将乙方右拳格开，右手随之握拳屈肘收抱于腰侧，拳心向上。（如图5-1-1所示）

图5-1-1

Fig.5-1-1

Shaolin quan is rich and varied in combat techniques. Its features include seamless transitions between moves, adaptability to changing circumstances, unpredictable offense and defense, strategic feints that disguise true intentions, and endless intricacies. In disadvantageous situations, traps can be set to lure the enemy and exploit their negligence. In this case, what appears weak may be strong, and what seems strong may be weak. Feints and genuine attacks may be intertwined, blurring the lines between true and false movements. In advantageous situations, the practitioner should display resolute intent, explosive power, and decisive actions, which fully showcases the features of Shaolin quan : robust strength, precise structure, clear rhythm, and profound skill. In actual combat, the techniques of Shaolin quan can be divided into long-range and close-range tactics. Long-range combat primarily utilizes punches and kicks, while close-range combat relies on body-to-body techniques. Close-range techniques involve using shoulders and hips in combination with knees and elbows to gain the upper hand.These techniques often create advantageous opportunities to disrupt the opponent's stance, force them into an indefensible position, and eventually subdue them.

I. Arhat Eighteen Hands in Actual Combat

1. Punch in Bow Stance

Movement Description: (The person in black is A, and the person in white is B)

(1) B: With the right foot in front and the left foot behind (or the left foot in front and the right foot behind), B swings the right fist forward from the right side to strike A's left ear. A: A immediately positions the left foot in front and the right foot behind, brings the left hand upward with the elbow bent, swings it to the left across the forehead and uses the radial side near the wrist of the forearm to parry B's right fist. Meanwhile, A clenches the right hand into a fist and positions it next to the right side of the waist, with the fist heart facing upward. (As shown in Fig. 5-1-1)

(2) Following the previous movement, A immediately turns to the left, straightens the right leg, and bends the left knee into a left bow stance. Next, A

（2）上动不停，甲方随即左转身，右腿伸直，左腿屈膝成左弓步；左拳屈肘收抱于左腰间，拳心向上，右拳向前平伸疾冲，击打乙方心窝，拳心向下，乙方为防被击伤稍后撤。（如图5-1-2所示）

动作要点：

（1）乙方掴击甲方左耳部，可能击打耳部上方的太阳穴（注：位于头部两侧，眼睛后部的凹陷处），也可能击打耳部下方的动脉。甲方的左拳格挡必须是根据对方的击打部位或向上迎或向下迎，高低不是固定不变，但是格挡一定要用近腕关节处的桡骨去磕击乙方腕关节处的桡骨。

（2）甲方使用“弓步冲拳”时拳的疾冲、右腿的后蹬、左拳的收抱，一定要在同一时间内完成，使冲拳借助蹬腿的地面反作用力更加迅速有力。同时击打的部位要准确，必须击中对手心窝（腹部胸骨剑突处）。

2. 马步架打

动作说明：

（1） 乙方：在甲方右脚在前、左脚在后站立的情况下，左脚向前，右脚在后（或右脚在前，左脚在后），用左拳从左外侧向前摆动掴击甲方右耳部，或太阳穴或颈动脉。甲方：立即右手握拳从身前屈肘向上，经额前向右绕环，用前臂近腕处尺骨一侧将乙方左拳格开，拳眼向左；左手随之握拳屈肘收抱于左腰侧，拳心向上；两腿呈右弓步。（如图5-1-3所示）

positions the left fist next to the left waist with the fist heart facing upward, and punches forward swiftly with the right fist, aiming at B's solar plexus with the fist heart facing downward. B retreats slightly to avoid being hurt. (As shown in Fig. 5-1-2)

图5-1-2
Fig.5-1-2

Key Points:

(1) When B attempts to attack A's left ear, the strike might target the temple above the ear (note: located on both sides of the head, in the depression behind the eyes) or the artery below the ear. A's block with the left fist must adapt to the opponent's target, either by raising it to meet an upward strike or lowering it to meet a downward strike. The height of the block is not fixed, but the block must use the radial bone near A's wrist joint to knock against the radial bone near B's wrist joint.

(2) When A performs the "Punch in Bow Stance", the rapid thrust of the punch, the backward push of the right leg, and the drawing back of the left fist must all be completed simultaneously. This coordination allows the punch to leverage the ground's reactive force from the leg push, making it faster and more powerful. Additionally, the strike must be precise, aiming at the opponent's solar plexus (the xiphoid process area of the abdominal sternum).

2. Block and Strike in Horse Stance

Movement Description:

(1) B: When A stands with the right foot in front and the left foot behind, B steps forward with the left foot in front and the right foot behind (or steps forward with the right foot in front and the left foot behind), and swings the left

图5–1–3
Fig.5–1–3

（2）上动未停，甲方随即左脚向前上一步，身体右转，两腿屈膝成马步；同时，左拳从腰间向左直臂平伸疾冲，击打乙方左肋下，拳心向下，乙方被击伤。（如图5–1–4所示）

动作要点：

（1）甲方使用“马步架打”，当左拳向前（左）平伸疾冲时，右臂肘必须在同一时间内向后（右）迅速拉回，凭借两臂的一冲一拉、向前向后的相互作用力，使冲拳更加迅猛。

（2）击打的部位可以是肾部，也可以是脾部，这要看乙方在向甲方进攻时哪一部位最容易被甲击中而定。

（3）“马步架打”可以根据乙方的攻势左右随机使用。

3. 弓步架打

动作说明：

（1）乙方：在甲方左脚前，右脚在后站立的情况下，乙方右脚向前（或左脚向前）用右拳从上向下劈砸甲方头顶。甲方：立即左手握拳从身前屈肘向上用前臂尺骨一侧将乙方右拳架阻，拳眼向下；同时右手握拳屈肘收抱于右腰侧，拳心向上；身体略向后移，两腿屈膝。

（2）上动不停，甲方随即上体左转，右腿蹬直，左脚屈膝成左弓

fist from the left side forward to strike A's right ear, temple, or carotid artery. A immediately clenches the right hand into a fist, brings it upward with the elbow bent, swings it to the right in front of the forehead, and uses the forearm near the wrist on the ulnar side to block B's left fist, with the fist eye facing the left. Next, A clenches the left hand into a fist, bends the elbow and positions it next to the left side of the waist, with the fist heart facing upward, and the legs in a right bow stance. (As shown in Fig. 5-1-3)

(2) Following previous movement, A immediately steps forward with the left foot, turns the body to the right, and bends both knees into horse stance. Simultaneously, A thrusts the left fist out straight from the waist to the left, striking below B's left rib, with the fist heart facing downward. (As shown in Fig. 5-1-4)

图5-1-4

Fig.5-1-4

Key Points:

(1) When A takes the block and strike in horse stance, as the left fist is thrusted swiftly forward (to the left), the right elbow must be quickly pulled back (to the right) at the same time. The simultaneous push and pull action of the arms, moving forward and backward, enhances the power and speed of the punch.

(2) The target area can be the kidney or the spleen, depending on which area of B is most exposed to A's strike during B's offensive move.

(3) The "Block and Strike in Horse Stance" can be used flexibly either to the

步，右拳向前平伸疾冲，击打乙方心窝，拳心向下，乙方即被击伤。（如图5-1-5所示）

图5-1-5
Fig.5-1-5

动作要点：

（1）甲方左拳前臂向上“架梁”阻格对方劈砸时，必须同时使上身略向后移，两腿微蹲，此时身向后移是为了闪避对方的拳势；腿微蹲是为了冲拳时便于蹬伸把身体和冲拳的力作用于地面，而后凭借反作用力使冲拳更有力。

（2）“弓步架打”根据乙方的拳势可以左右使用，要灵活出招，随势应势。

4. 搂手磕打

动作说明：

（1）乙方：在甲方左脚在前、右脚在后站立的情况下，乙方右脚向前用右拳从上向下劈砸甲方头部。（如图5-1-6所示）

left or right according to B's attack.

3. Block and Strike in Bow Stance

Movement Description:

(1) With A standing with the left foot in front and the right foot behind, B steps forward with the right foot (or the left foot) and chops down with the right fist from above toward the top of A's head. A immediately clenches the left hand into a fist, raises the bent elbow from in front of the body, and blocks B's right fist with the forearm on the ulnar side, with the fist eye facing downward. Meanwhile, A clenches the right hand into a fist with the elbow bent; positions it next to the right side of the waist with the fist heart facing upward; and moves the body slightly backward, with both knees bent.

(2) Following the previous movement, A then turns the upper body to the left, straightens the right leg, bends the left knee into a left bow stance, and throw a swift and straight right-hand fist at B's precordium, with the fist heart facing downward. (As shown in Fig. 5-1-5)

Key Points:

(1) When raising the left forearm to block the opponent's attack, A must simultaneously slightly move the upper body backward and slightly bend both knees. The backward movement is to dodge the opponent's fist; and the bending of the knees is to push off the ground, use the force of the body and the punch against the ground, and then leverage the reactive force to make the punch more powerful.

(2) In response to B's attack, the "Block and Strike in Bow Stance" can be done in either left bow stance or right bow stance, which requires both flexibility and adaptability.

4. Seize Hand and Strike

Movement Description:

(1) B: With A standing with the left foot in front and the right foot behind, B steps forward with the right foot and chops at A's head with the right fist. (As shown in Fig. 5-1-6)

(2) A: A immediately leans the upper body backward to dodge B's chop. Then, A lifts the left hand from the body side with the elbow bent, seizes B's right wrist, and presses it down with the thumb facing inward. Meanwhile, A clenches right

图5-1-6

Fig.5-1-6

（2）甲方：立即使上体后闪，避开乙方的劈砸；同时，左手从左侧向上屈肘绕环抄起，在额前向里、向下将乙方右拳腕部搂住下按，拇指一侧向内，右手握拳从身前屈肘提起，拳心向下。上动未停，甲方继续搂住乙方右拳腕向下按，右拳由左臂里侧向上，向前绕环翻起，用拳背前缘边部磕击乙方前额，拳心向上；上体随之向前逼近乙方，右臂也随势由屈到伸；乙方即被击伤。（如图5-1-7所示）

动作要点：

（1）闪身、搂手、磕打的动作要迅速连贯，中间不能有丝毫停顿。否则对方在右腕被搂后，左拳将会乘隙进攻。

（2）右拳磕打，须注意腕肘不能僵劲，应该像抽鞭子似的将前臂、拳手甩出；特别是腕关节，在右拳从身前屈肘提起时，也须向拳心一面屈起，这样便于磕打时甩腕。

（3）搂打的部位以对方的前额眉间为宜。

（4）“搂手磕打”也可以根据对方的拳势左右使用，以下各手都是如此，不再说明。

hand into a fist and lifts it from the front of the body with the elbow bent, and the fist heart facing downward. Without any pause, A continues to press down on B's right wrist while flipping the right fist upward and forward from beneath the left arm and striking B's forehead with the front edge of the fist back. Next, A moves the upper body forward to approach B, with the right arm extending from bent to straight. (As shown in Fig. 5-1-7)

图5-1-7

Fig. 5-1-7

Key Points:

(1) The movements of dodging, seizing, and striking must be quick and continuous, without any pause in between. Otherwise, after their right wrist is seized, the opponent may avail the opportunity to attack.

(2) When striking with the right fist, be sure that the wrist and elbow are not stiff. The forearm and fist should be swung out like a whip. The wrist joint should be bent toward the fist heart when the right fist is raised in front of the body with the elbow bent. This facilitates a flick of the wrist during the strike.

(3) The target area for the strike should ideally be the opponent's forehead between the eyebrows.

(4) In response to the opponent's attack, the "Seize Hand and Strike" can be adapted to either the left side or right side, as with the other techniques described above. This point will not be repeated in the rest of this chapter.

5. 托肘穿打

动作说明：

（1）甲方：左脚在前，右脚在后站立（或左脚在前，右脚在后站立），当乙方左弓步用左拳向甲头顶劈砸时，甲用左手向上将乙方左臂肘托起。（如图5-1-8所示）

图5-1-8

Fig. 5-1-8

（2）上动未停，甲方随即用右拳向前平伸疾冲，击打乙方左肋下方，拳心向下；同时，左手握拳向左肩处收回，拳心向下；乙方即被击伤。（如图5-1-9所示）

动作要点：

（1）使用“托肘穿打”这一手，托肘、出击必须快速贯串一气。托肘或出击迟缓，都会给对方造成有隙可乘的机会。

（2）托肘的部位，一定要托在对方上臂接近肘关节的地方，这样对方就失去了向下压的力量。如果托对方的前臂就难以收到应有的效果。

5. Lift Elbow and Punch Through

Movement Description:

(1)A: A stands with the left foot in front and the right foot behind (or stands with the left foot in front and the right foot behind). When B, in a left bow stance, chops at A's head with the left fist, A uses the left hand to lift B's left arm. (As shown in Fig. 5-1-8)

(2) Following the previous movement, A then punches forward with the right fist, and strikes the area below B's left rib with the fist heart facing down. Meanwhile, A clenches the left hand into a fist and pulls it back toward the left shoulder, with the fist heart facing down. (As shown in Fig. 5-1-9)

图5-1-9

Fig. 5-1-9

Key Points:

(1) When executing the "Lift Elbow and Punch Through" technique, the action of lifting the elbow and punching must be performed quickly and fluidly in one continuous motion. Any delay in lifting the elbow or in punching can give the opponent an opportunity to exploit.

(2) The elbow must be lifted via the upper arm close to the opponent's elbow joint, rendering the opponent unable to exert downward pressure. On the contrary, lifting the opponent's forearm would likely not achieve the desired effect.

6. 弓步顶肘

动作说明：

（1）乙方：在甲方左脚在前、右脚在后站立的情况下，乙右脚向前用右拳从右外侧向前摆动横掴甲方左耳部。甲方：立即左手握拳从身前屈肘向上，经额前向左绕环，臂内旋用前臂近腕处的尺骨一侧将乙方右拳格开；右手随之握拳屈肘收抱于右腰侧，拳心向上。（如图5-1-10所示）

图5-1-10

Fig. 5-1-10

（2）上动未停，甲方随即身躯左转，左腿屈膝，右腿伸直，成左弓步；同时，右臂盘肘用肘尖向前顶出，击打乙方右胸乳下肋骨部位；右拳则顺势移于左肩前，拳心向下；乙方即被击伤。（如图5-1-11所示）

动作要点：

（1）肘尖前顶时要注意防止肩向上耸起，耸肩会削弱顶肘的力量，一定要使肩向下沉。

（2）顶肘的击打部位一定是接近乳部的下方，如果是乳部的上方则击打的效果不大。

6. Elbow Strike in Bow Stance

Movement Description:

(1)B : While A stands with the left foot in front and the right foot behind, B steps forward with the right foot and swings the right fist from the outside to attack A's left ear. A : A immediately clenches the left hand into a fist, bends the elbow upward from the front of the body, swings the fist to the left across the forehead, and rotates the arm to block B's right fist with the ulnar side near the wrist of the forearm. Meanwhile, A clenches the right hand into a fist, bends the elbow, and pulls it back to the right side of the waist, with the fist heart facing upward.

(2) Following the previous movement, A immediately turns the body to the left, bends the left leg at the knee, and straightens the right leg, forming a left bow stance. Meanwhile, A thrusts the right elbow forward with the tip of the elbow hitting the lower ribcage of B's right chest. A then brings the right fist in front of the left shoulder, with the fist heart facing downward. (As shown in Fig. 5-1-11)

图5-1-11

Fig. 5-1-11

Key Points:

(1) When thrusting forward with the tip of the elbow, be careful not to shrug the shoulder, as shrugging will weaken the power of the elbow strike. It is crucial to maintain a downward sinking force in the shoulder.

(2) The target area of the elbow strike must be close to the lower part of the chest. If it is above the chest, the effectiveness of the strike will be significantly

8. 切掌击腿

动作说明：

（1）乙方：在甲方左脚在前、右脚在后的情况下，乙用右脚踢击甲方裆部或小腹（如图5-1-12所示）

图5-1-12

Fig. 5-1-12

（2）甲方：立即使右脚后撤，身躯右转，闪开乙方的右脚；同时，右手从下直臂向右、向上架举于头顶右上方；左手从下屈肘向左、向上，由左耳侧向前、向下绕环，用小指一侧劈砍乙方右脚胫骨，掌指向前，拇指一侧向上，两腿随势屈膝略下蹲，乙方即被击伤。（如图5-1-13所示）

动作要点：

（1）撤步、转身、举掌、劈掌等动作，必须在同一时间内一气呵成，中间不能有丝毫停顿。

（2）劈切的部位根据实际情况可以劈对方小腿的胫骨，也可以劈其脚背或踝关节的前面。

reduced.

8. Palm Chopping and Leg Kicking

Movement Description:

(1) B: When A stands with the left foot in front and the right foot behind, B kicks toward A's groin or lower abdomen with the right foot.

(2) A: A immediately steps back with the right foot, turns the body to the right, and dodges B's right foot. Meanwhile, A raises the right hand straight up and to the right, lifting it above the head to the upper right. A also bends the right arm at the elbow, moves the left hand left and upward, circles it from the side of the left ear forward and downward, and strikes the shin of B's right foot with the ulnar side of the hand, with the palm facing forward, thumb side facing upward, and both legs bent slightly at the knees. (As shown in Fig. 5-1-13)

图5-1-13

Fig. 5-1-13

Key Points:

(1) The actions including stepping back, turning, raising the palm, and chopping must be executed smoothly and continuously without any pause.

(2) The target area of the chop can vary based on the actual situation. It can be the shin of the lower leg, the top of the foot, or the front of the ankle joint.

9. Double Palm Push

Movement Description:

9. 分掌双推

动作说明：

（1）乙方：在甲方左脚在前、右脚在后站立的情况下，乙方两拳（或两掌）从左右两侧向前打甲方两耳。甲方：在乙方两拳（两掌）即将接近两耳时，迅速使右脚从身后屈膝提起，两手从下屈肘向前，由乙两臂中间向上弧形绕环，臂外旋用前臂靠近腕处的桡骨一侧向外磕击乙方两腕臂骨，将乙方的两拳（两掌）格开，掌指向上，掌背向前。（如图5-1-14所示）

图5-1-14
Fig. 5-1-14

（2）上动未停，甲方随即使右脚向乙方裆间上步插进，左腿屈膝，右腿伸直，成右弓步；同时，两掌臂内旋使掌心向前，向乙方胸部贴靠，上动未停，甲方两臂伸直，用两掌将乙方推出。（如图5-1-15所示）

动作要点：

（1）双掌外分磕击对方两腕骨时，要注意两肘不要撑开，仅用前臂向外分；同时外分的幅度也不要太宽，微超过肩宽即可。

（2）右脚插向对方裆前，必使身体向前逼近对方，两掌屈肘将对方靠住；而后左腿后蹬，两臂由屈到伸，凭借地面的反作用力才能将对方推倒。

(1)B: When A stands with the left foot in front and the right foot behind, B attacks A's ears from both sides with both fists (or plams). A : As B's fists (or plams) are about to reach A's ears, A quickly lifts the right knee up from behind, brings both hands forward from below with the elbows bent, and makes an upward arc through the middle of B's arms. A then rotates the arms outward and uses the forearm near the wrist, specifically the radial side, to knock outward against B's wrists, blocking B's fists (or palms) with the fingers upward and the plam backs forward. (As shown in Fig. 5-1-14)

(2)With no pause, A immediately steps forward with the right foot toward B's groin area. The left knee is bent and the right knee is straightened, forming a right bow stance. Simultaneously, rotate both arms inward so that the palms face forward and press against B's chest area. Without any pause, A extends both arms and uses the palms to push B away. (As shown in Fig. 5-1-15)

图5-1-15

Fig. 5-1-15

Key Points:

(1) When knocking against the opponent's wrists with both palms, it is critical to keep the elbows from flaring out. Be sure to only use the forearms to separate outward. Also, the extent of the outward separation should not be too wide, just slightly wider than shoulder width.

(2) When stepping toward the opponent's groin with the right foot, ensure the body moves forward to approach the opponent closely and both palms press against the opponent with elbows bent. Then, push back with the left leg, and extend both arms from bent to straight, relying on the ground's reaction force to

（3）当身、步、双掌逼近对方时，如果能够趁对方急欲向后退避的一瞬间，蹬腿发掌，对方定会被跌得更重。

（4）两掌贴靠推击的部位能够在对方的乳下两肋处更好。

10. 挂腿勾挑

动作说明：

（1）乙方：在甲方左脚在前、右脚在后站立的情况下，左脚向前用左拳直打甲方鼻部，或脸面的其他部位。甲方：立即使左手从下屈肘经身前向右、向上，由脸前向左弧形绕环，在鼻前，手臂内旋将乙方左拳腕部抓住。

（2）上动未停，甲方随之使左脚尖外展，身躯半面向左转，右脚屈膝在身后离地提起，右手从下屈肘向右、向上弧形绕环举于胸部前方，抓住乙左后臂。上动未停，甲方右脚向乙方左腿外侧接近踝关节处踢去，将乙方左腿挂住向身前勾挑，脚尖向上。（如图5-1-16所示）

图5-1-16

Fig. 5-1-16

动作要点：

（1）勾挂对方腿部时，必须利用小腿的摆踢力量，边踢边向上勾

push the opponent down.

(3) If one can take advantage of the moment when the opponent is eager to retreat, by pushing with the leg and striking with the palms, the opponent will surely fall even harder.

10. Hanging Leg Hook and Lift

Movment Description:

(1) B: While A stands with the left foot in front and the right foot behind, B steps forward with the left foot and throws a straight punch with the left fist toward A's nose or another part of the face. A: A immediately lifts the left hand from below, and moves it in front of the body toward the right and up, creating an arc from in front of the face to the left. In front of the nose, A rotates the arm inward to grab B's left fist at the wrist.

(2) Without any pause, A then points the left toes outward, half-turns the torso to the left, and lifts the right knee off the ground from behind. Meanwhile, A moves the right hand in an upward arc from below to the front of the chest, and grabs B's left rear arm. Next, A immediately kicks toward the outside of B's left leg near the ankle, and hooks B's left leg to lift it forward with the toes pointing up.(As shown in Fig. 5-1-16)

Key Points:

(1) When hooking the opponent's leg, it is crucial to utilize the swinging force of the lower leg. The coordination between the upward and downward motions must be synchronized in speed to achieve better results.

(2) The hook should target close to the ankle joint, not too high, as this makes it easier to bring the opponent down.

挑，同时上下动作还须快慢一致，才能获得较好的效果。

（2）挂勾的部位一定要在踝关节近处，不能太高，这样易于踢倒对方。

11. 伏身后扫

动作说明：

（1）乙方：当甲方左脚在前、右脚在后站立的情况下，乙右脚向前用右拳击打甲方腹部。（如图5-1-17所示）

图5-1-17

Fig. 5-1-17

（2）甲方：在乙方右拳击来时迅速左腿屈膝全蹲，左脚跟离地掀起，右腿伸直向右后方仆地，两手向右脚前扶地，以左脚掌辗地为轴，摆臂转腰使右脚贴地向后扫，用小腿后面接近脚跟部位扫荡乙方的双腿，将乙方扫到。（如图5-1-18所示）

动作要点：

（1）“扫堂腿”的力量来源于速度力量，这就需要在俯身时，身躯和两臂猛然用力向右下方拧腰摆臂转动；同时，左脚跟也须与拧腰摆臂配合一致向外展。

（2）扫转时右脚一定要贴着地面，但又不要贴得太紧；身躯和右腿始终保持小于直角的角度，不要大于直角。

（3）使用“扫堂腿”后扫时，不论对方是击腹或击脸，只要是正

11.Ducking and Sweeping Behind

Movement Description:

(1) B: When A stands with the left foot in front and the right foot behind, B steps forward with the right foot and strikes A's abdomen with the right fist.(As shown in Fig. 5-1-17)

(2) A: As B's right fist comes in, A quickly bends the left leg at the knee into a full squat, lifts the left heel off the ground, extends the right leg straight toward the back right to stay close to the ground, and places both hands in front of the right foot to support the body on the ground. Taking the left foot's sole as a pivot on the ground, A swings the arms and twists the waist to sweep backward with the right foot close to the ground, using the back of the lower leg near the heel to sweep B's legs, and bring B down. (As shown in Fig. 5-1-18)

图5-1-18

Fig. 5-1-18

Key Points:

(1) The force of the "sweeping leg" comes from speed and strength, which requires a sudden forceful twist of the torso and arms toward the right lower side while ducking. Simultaneously, the left heel must also expand outward in coordination with the twisting of the torso and the swinging of the arms.

(2) During the sweeping, the right foot must stay close to the ground but not too close; the torso and the right leg should always maintain an angle less than 90 degrees, not greater.

(3) When using the "sweeping leg" technique, regardless of whether the opponent is striking the abdomen or the face, as long as they are lunging forward,

面扑来，都必须和对方一起动，脚步向前移动之机立即俯身迅速扫转，不能像图中所示的那样待对方已打到近身时才开始扫转。

12. 弹腿踢击

动作说明：

当乙方向甲方正面作任何进攻时，甲方即用右脚（或左脚）使脚面绷平、脚尖向前向乙方胫骨、裆部或小腹踢击。（如图5-1-19所示）

图5-1-19
Fig. 5-1-19

动作要点：

（1）向前弹踢，必须先使小腿向身后屈膝将脚离地提起，而后绷平脚面，五趾用力下抓，使小腿用力迅速向前弹出，像向前踢球那样踢出，不应将小腿向后屈起与用力向前摆荡的两个部分机械地分割开来，须连成一气。

（2）弹踢不宜超过水平部位。踢对方小腿胫骨时，还须使支撑腿屈膝稍做下踢才好。

13. 叉掌锁喉

动作说明：

（1）乙方：当甲方左脚在前、右脚在后站立的情况下，右脚向前

one must move together with the opponent. One should immediately bend down and swiftly sweep. One cannot wait until the opponent is close, as shown in the illustration, to begin the sweep.

12. Snap Kick

Movement Description:

When B makes any frontal attack on A, A immediately uses the right foot (or left foot) with the instep flat and toes pointing forward to kick at B's shin, groin, or lower abdomen. (As shown in Fig. 5-1-19)

Key Points:

(1) To perform a forward snap kick, bend the lower leg backward at the knee to lift the foot off the ground. Then, straighten the instep, extending the toes forcefully forward from back to front. However, be sure to seamlessly connect the two parts of bending the lower leg backward and swinging it forward with force.

(2) The snap kick should not exceed the horizontal level. When kicking the opponent's shin, it is also necessary to slightly bend the supporting leg and perform a downward kick for better execution.

13.Cross Palm Lock Throat

Movement Description:

(1) B: When A stands with the left foot in front and the right foot behind, B punches A's chest using the right fist with the right foot in front (or the left foot in front). A: A immediately blocks the punch by moving the left arm to the right and upward with the elbow bent.(As shown in Fig. 5-1-20)

(2) Following previous movement, A grabs B's right wrist, rotates the arm to turn the palm upward, and twists B's right arm inward and upward. At the same time, A steps forward with the right foot, keeps the four fingers of the right hand together with the palm facing up, and extends the arm straight forward and upward from the right side of the waist, striking B's throat with the fingertips.(As shown in Fig. 5-1-21)

（或左脚向前）用右拳向甲方胸部击打。甲方：立即使左手由身前屈肘向右、向上格挡。（如图5-1-20所示）

图5-1-20

Fig. 5-1-20

（2）上动不停，甲方抓住乙方右拳腕，手臂外旋使手心向上将乙方右臂向里向上扭转；同时，右脚向前上步，右手四指并拢，掌心向上，由右腰侧直臂向前上伸出，用指尖击打乙方咽喉。（如图5-1-21所示）

动作要点：

使用本招时，如果目的在于将对方卡跌，在卡喉时则须将对方的拳腕松开让其后仰跌倒；拇指和其余四指收紧，这样才能更有穿刺击打的力量。

14. 挎肘撅臂

动作说明：

（1）乙方：当甲方左脚在前、右脚在后站立的情况下，乙右脚向前（或左脚向前）用右拳直臂向前击打甲方胸腹。甲方：左手从乙方右拳臂的下面屈肘向右、向上、向左弧形绕环，臂内旋将乙方右拳肘部抓住，手心向下，拇指一侧向前。（如图5-1-22所示）

图5-1-21

Fig. 5-1-21

Key Points:

When using this technique, if the goal is to make the opponent fall, one should release the opponent's wrist when locking their throat to allow them to fall backward. The thumb and the other four fingers should be tightened to increase the penetrating force of the strike.

14. Elbow Hook and Arm Lever

Movement Description:

(1) B: When A stands with the left foot in front and the right foot behind, B steps forward with the right foot (or left foot) and strikes forward with a straight right fist toward A's chest and abdomen. A: A moves the left hand from under B's right arm to the right, upward, then to the left in an arc, and rotates the arm internally to grab B's right elbow with the palm facing down and the thumb side forward.(As shown in Fig. 5-1-22)

(2) Following the previous movement, A grabs B's right wrist, and rotates the arm outward with the palm facing upward to turn B's right arm outward. Simultaneously, A steps forward with the right foot, turns the upper body to the left, clenches the right hand into a fist, circles it from under B's right arm to the front, uses the elbow to hook behind B's elbow joint, and forcefully lifts it upward, while firmly grabbing B's right wrist and pressing it downward hard, and levers B's right arm to injure the elbow in a combined upward and downward motion.(As shown in Fig. 5-1-23)

图5-1-22

Fig. 5-1-22

（2）上动不停，甲方抓住乙方右拳腕部，臂外旋使手心向上将乙方右臂向外扭转；同时，右脚向前跨步，上体随之左转，右手握拳从乙方右臂下面屈肘向身前绕环抄起，用肘弯挎住乙方肘关节的后面用力向上抄，左手即抓牢乙方右拳腕部用力向下压，一上一下扳撅乙方右臂肘受伤。（如图5-1-23所示）

动作要点：

（1）撅臂的动作必须快速，用力要干脆；右肘的抄挎和左手的压扳，一定要在一瞬之间上下一起用力。

（2）撅臂一定不要硬扳，当对方已经觉察而及时将臂肘屈起，使你无法扭转和扳撅的时候，就不用再硬扭硬撅。

（3）使用本势，要收到撅臂的效果，关键还在于搂腕时的扭臂。当将对方的拳腕抓住之后，须紧紧抓牢迅速用力向外扭转其臂，使对方无法在扭臂之前将臂肘屈起。

15. 缠手截腕

动作说明：

（1）乙方：右脚向前（或左脚向前），用右手向甲方当胸抓去。（如图5-1-24所示）

图5-1-23

Fig. 5-1-23

Key Points:

(1) The action of levering the arm must be quick, and the force must be decisive; the hooking of the right elbow and the pressing with the left hand must be done simultaneously swiftly with combined upward and downward force.

(2) Do not forcefully lever the arm. If the opponent finds the intention and bends their elbow in time, making it impossible for you to twist and lever, do not continue to force it.

(3) The key to achieving the effect of this move lies in the twisting of the arm when grabbing the wrist. After grabbing the opponent's wrist, one must firmly and quickly twist their arm outward, preventing them from bending their elbow before one can twist and lever it.

15. Entwining Hand and Intercepting Wrist

Movement Description:

(1) B: B steps forward with the right foot (or left foot), and reach out with the right hand to grab toward A's chest.(As shown in Fig. 5-1-24)

(2) A: A firmly grasps B's right hand with the left hand. With the edge of the right palm near the little finger against B's wrist joint from above, A moves the right hand outward, downward, and inward in an entwining motion and subsequently rotates the right arm outward to injure B's wrist joint. (As shown in Fig. 5-1-25)

图5-1-24
Fig. 5-1-24

（2）甲方：甲方左手握牢乙方右手；用右掌小指一侧的边缘部分切着乙方的腕关节，由上向外、向下、向里缠绕，右臂随之外旋；乙方腕关节即被截伤。（如图5-1-25所示）

动作要点：

使用本势时，必须一手将对方抓臂的手握紧不放，另一手用小指一侧的掌缘从对方腕关节的尺侧端（豌豆骨和尺骨的接缝间）切入，顺其关节紧紧缠绕，破坏和扭伤腕关节的韧带与肌腱，重则使腕关节脱臼。

16. 缠肘截腕

动作说明：

（1）乙方：左脚向前，左手臂内旋拇指一侧向下，反手将甲方接近腕关节处的前臂抓住，准备进攻甲方。（如图5-1-26所示）

图5-1-25

Fig. 5-1-25

Key Points:

When using this technique, one must firmly grasp the opponent's arm-grabbing hand, while using the edge of the palm near the little finger of the other hand to slice into the opponent's wrist joint from the ulnar side (between the pisiform and the ulna), and tightly entwine along the joint, damage and twist the ligaments and tendons of the wrist joint, and potentially cause dislocation in severe cases.

16.Entangling Elbow and Intercepting Wrist

Movement Description:

(1)B: B steps forward with the left foot, rotates the left arm inward so that the thumb side faces downward, and grabs A's forearm near the wrist with a reverse grip, preparing to attack A. (As illustrated in Fig. 5-1-26)

(2)A: A quickly lifts the right arm with the elbow bent and clenches the right hand into a fist, with the fist heart facing downward. Simultaneously, A stretches the left hand over the back of B's hand to firmly grasp B's left hand, gripping B's index, middle, ring, and little fingers with the thumb, and gripping the edge of B's hand near the little finger with the other four fingers. With no pause, A then firmly grasps B's left hand with the left hand, and uses the forearm of the right hand to press down on B's left wrist, wrapping and entangling it inward, forward, and downward; at the same time, A also leans the upper body forward and

图5-1-26
Fig. 5-1-26

（2）甲方：迅速使右臂屈肘向上提起，右手随之握拳，拳心斜向下；同时，用左手伸向乙方手背上面将乙方左手握牢，拇指握紧乙方左手的食指、中指、无名指和小指，而其余四指则并拢握紧乙方左手小指一侧的边缘。上动不停，甲方随即左手握牢乙方左手，用右手的前臂压紧乙方的左腕关节向里、向前、向下绕环缠裹；同时，上体也向前、向下倾俯逼近；乙方即受伤倒地。（如图5-1-27所示）

动作要点：

缠肘截腕则是用前臂骨压紧对方的腕关节进行缠裹。

17. 沉肘截腕

动作说明：

（1）乙方：右脚向前，用右手抓拿甲方左肩的上方部位。甲方：迅速使右手伸向乙方右手背的上面将乙方右手握牢，拇指压抓乙方右手掌指，其余四指并拢握紧乙方右手；同时，上体后移将乙方右手向后带。（如图5-1-28所示）

downward to press in; resulting in B being injured and falling to the ground. (As illustrated in Fig. 5-1-27)

图5-1-27
Fig. 5-1-27

Key Points:

The technique of "Entangling Elbow and Intercepting Wrist" involves using the forearm bone to press tightly against the opponent's wrist joint for wrapping and entanglement.

17.Sinking Elbow and Intercepting Wrist

Movement Description:

(1) B: B steps forward with the right foot, using the right hand to grab the upper part of A's left shoulder. A: A quickly extends the right hand over the back of B's right hand to firmly grasp it, gripping B's palm fingers with the thumb and B's right hand with the other four fingers. Meanwhile, A moves the upper body backward, pulling B's right hand backward. (As shown in Fig. 5-1-28)

(2) With no pause, A then turns the upper body to the right, with the right elbow hanging down, tightly holds B's right hand, and twists it downward in front of the body. At the same time, A clenches the left hand into a fist, places the elbow above B's right arm, and presses down forcefully with the elbow, with the fist heart facing behind. Next, A continues to lower the left elbow and presses down on B's right elbow with the upper arm behind the elbow. While pressing down, A bends both knees in a squat and lowers the center of gravity. (As illustrated in Fig. 5-1-29)

图5-1-28

Fig. 5-1-28

（2）上动未停，甲方随即上体右转，右肘向下垂，用右手握紧乙方的右手向身前、向下扳拧；同时，左手握拳使肘处于乙方右臂的上面，向下用力按压，拳心朝向身后。上动未停，甲方继续使左肘下沉，用肘后的上臂向下压砸乙方右手的肘关节；在压砸的同时，两腿屈膝下蹲，重心下沉。（如图5-1-29所示）

动作要点：

本势沉肘截腕的要领，也还是在于缠裹，两腿屈膝，身躯重心下沉是加重对方腕关节的压力，身躯向左转动则是助长左上臂压肘的螺旋之势。因此，屈膝、重心下沉，必须和向下压肘的动作一致起来。

二、连环拳实战技法

1. 起势

动作说明：（穿红色衣者为甲，穿白衣者为乙）

（1）甲乙并步直立,两掌垂放于身体两侧；目视前方。（如图5-2-1所示）

图5-1-29

Fig. 5-1-29

Key Points:

The key of the "Sinking Elbow and Intercepting Wrist" technique is still in the wrapping and entangling. Bending both knees and lowering the body's center of gravity increases the pressure on the opponent's wrist joint. Turning the body to the left enhances the spiral motion of pressing the elbow with the left upper arm. Therefore, bending the knees, sinking the center of gravity, and pressing down with the elbow must be coordinated together.

II. Interlinked Fist in Actual Combat

1. Starting Position

Movement Description:(The person in red is A, and the person in white is B)

(1) A and B stand side by side, with both palms hanging by the body sides. Gaze straight ahead. (As shown in Fig. 5-2-1)

(2) Both A and B hold their fists at their waists while looking into each other's eyes. (As shown in Fig. 5-2-2)

图5-2-1

Fig. 5-2-1

（2）甲、乙两拳抱于腰间，同时注视对方双眼。（如图5-2-2所示）

动作要点：

起势动作整洁有力，体态端正。

2. 乙左弓步右冲拳，甲左格冲心拳

动作说明：

（1）乙右转90度，左腿向前上步成左弓步，左拳抱于腰间，同时冲右拳击打甲面部。（如图5-2-3所示）

（2）甲左脚向左开步成马步，右拳抱于腰间，同时左臂向左格挡乙右冲拳并迅速抓握乙右手臂向下按压，甲上动不停，变左弓步右冲拳，击打乙方心窝，注视对方双眼。（如图5-2-4所示）

图5-2-2

Fig. 5-2-2

Key Points:

The starting movement is neat and forceful, with an upright posture.

2. B's Right Punch in Left Bow Stance, A's Left Block and Heart Piercing Punch

Movement Description:

(1) B turns 90 degrees to the right, steps forward with the left leg into a left bow stance, holds the left fist at the waist, and punches with the right fist toward A's face. (As shown in Fig. 5-2-3)

(2) A steps to the left with the left foot into a horse stance, holds the right fist at the waist, and uses the left arm to block B's right punch to the left, and quickly grabs and presses down B's right arm. Without any pause, A switches to a left bow stance and punches with the right fist toward B's chest, while looking into the opponent's eyes. (As shown in Fig. 5-2-4)

图5-2-3

Fig. 5-2-3

动作要点：

冲拳与格挡协调一致，同时完成，把握格挡时机。

3. 甲十字蹬腿，乙回身抱头

动作说明：

甲接上式，右脚提起向前弹蹬乙腹部，同时右拳拳心朝上收回腰间,左拳拳心朝下向前冲出，臂与肩平，力达左拳，目视乙方双眼。乙身体右转90度成右弓步，双臂成抱头式，同时左臂向上挑开甲右腿，目视甲方双眼。（如图5-2-5所示）

图5-2-5

Fig. 5-2-5

图5-2-4

Fig. 5-2-4

Key Points:

The punch and block are coordinated and executed simultaneously, with the block precisely timed.

3. A's Cross Kick, B's Turning Around and Covering Head

Movement Description:

Following the previous movement, A lifts the right foot and kicks forward toward B's abdomen, while pulling back the right fist to the waist with the fist heart facing upward, and punching the left fist forward with the fist heart facing down. A then keeps the arm level with the shoulder, directs force through to the left fist, and looks into B's eyes. B turns the body 90 degrees to the right into a right bow stance, with arms in a head-covering position, while lifting the left arm to block A's right leg, and looking into A's eyes. (As shown in Fig. 5-2-5)

Key Points:

A makes sure the supporting leg is stable, with force directed to the heel of the right leg. B turns around quickly, with the left arm raised to lift the ankle joint of A's right leg.

动作要点：

甲左支撑腿稳定，右腿力达脚跟；乙回身迅速，左臂上托甲右腿踝关节处。

4. 甲马步冲拳，乙弓步顶肘

动作说明：

甲身体左转90度，右脚向右落地成马步，双脚平行，双膝外展，双腿下蹲。同时，左拳拳心朝上收回腰间，右拳拳心朝下向右冲出，臂与肩平，力达右拳。向右摆头，目视右方。乙右腿向前上步成右弓步，左手抓握甲右手腕，同时右肘顶击甲右肋部。（如图5-2-6所示）

动作要点：

甲力达拳面；乙力达肘尖。

5. 乙左站立冲拳，甲马步架打

动作说明：

乙上左步成左站立步同时冲左拳击打甲头部，目视甲双眼。甲身体右后转180度，双脚跳步成马步，双脚平行，双膝外展。同时，甲方右拳经胸前再向上架起乙方左拳于甲方头顶上方，左拳心朝下向左冲出击打乙心窝，力达左拳，目视乙心窝。（如图4-2-7所示）

图5-2-7

Fig. 5-2-7

4. A's Punch in Horse Stance, B's Elbow Strike in Bow Stance

Movement Description:

A turns the body 90 degrees to the left, steps the right foot to the right into a horse stance, and keeps the feet parallel, the knees pointing outward, both legs bent. Simultaneously, A pulls back the left fist to the waist with the fist heart facing upward, and punches the right fist out to the right with the fist heart facing down, the arm level with the shoulder, and the force directed through to the right fist. A turns the head to the right and gazes to the right. B steps forward with the right leg into a right bow stance, grabs A's right wrist with the left hand, and thrusts the right elbow toward A's right rib. (As shown in Fig. 5-2-6)

图5-2-6

Fig. 5-2-6

Key Points:

A directs force through to the fist; B directs force through to the tip of the elbow.

5. B's Left Standing Punch, A's Block and Strike in Horse Stance

Movement Description:

B steps forward with the left foot into a left standing stance while punching with the left fist toward A's head, and looking into A's eyes. A turns the body 180 degrees to the right rear, jumping into a horse stance, with feet parallel and knees pointing outward. Simultaneously, A moves the right fist across the chest and then upward to block B's left fist above A's head, while punching out with the left fist toward B's chest, with force directed through the left fist and eyes on B's chest.

动作要点：

乙左手左脚击打同时到位，甲转身跳步落地稳固，先架后冲，左拳力达乙心窝。

6. 甲左弓步左推掌，乙右弓步右格挡

动作说明：

甲上步成左弓步，同时左手变立掌向前推出击打乙面部，右拳拳心朝上收于腰间，力达左掌根，目视乙双眼。乙退左步成右弓步，同时左拳拳心朝上收回腰间，右掌向右格挡甲左推掌，目视甲双眼。（如图5-2-8所示）

动作要点：

甲推掌与乙格掌同步完成，协调一致。

7. 甲左弓步右推掌，乙左弓步左格挡

动作说明：

甲左掌收回腰间掌心朝上，同时右手变立掌向前推出击打乙面部，力达右掌根，目视乙双眼。乙换步成左弓步，同时左手变掌向左格挡甲右推掌，右掌掌心朝上收回腰间，目视甲双眼。（如图5-2-9所示）

图5-2-9
Fig. 5-2-9

动作要点：

甲右推掌力达掌根，乙迅速换步，左掌格挡甲右推掌，动作协调

(As shown in Fig. 4-2-7)

Key Points:

Strikes from B's left hand and left foot should be simultaneous. A needs to turn and jump into a stable landing, blocking before striking, with the force of the left fist directed to B's chest.

6. A's Left Palm Push in Left Bow Stance, B's Right Block in Right Bow Stance

Movement Description:

A steps forward into a left bow stance, simultaneously changes the left hand to an upright palm and pushes it forward to strike B's face. Next A pulls back the right fist to the waist with the fist heart facing upward, force directed through to the base of the left palm and the eyes on B's eyes. B steps back with the left foot into a right bow stance, and pulls back the left fist to the waist with the fist heart facing upward, the right palm blocking A's left palm push, and the eyes on A's eyes. (As shown in Fig. 5-2-8)

图5-2-8

Fig. 5-2-8

Key Points:

A's palm push and B's palm block are synchronized and coordinated.

7. A's Right Palm Push in Left Bow Stance, B's Left Block in Left Bow Stance

Movement Description:

A pulls back the left palm to the waist with the palm facing upward, while switching the right hand to an upright palm and pushes it forward to strike B's

一致。

8. 乙抱拳蹬腿，甲仆步勾手

动作说明：

乙双手抱拳收回腰间，同时提起左脚弹蹬甲裆部，目视甲双眼。甲身体右转90度，右腿屈膝全蹲成左仆步。同时右掌下落，经右膝前向后变勾手，指尖儿向上背于腰后部。左臂向左经面部与右臂相应运行，立掌放于右肩前，目视乙双眼。（如图5-2-10所示）

图5-2-10

Fig. 5-2-10

动作要点：

甲转身成仆步迅速，避开乙右脚；乙力达脚跟，眼睛有神。

9. 乙右弓步双贯拳，甲独立步双开门

动作说明：

乙右腿落步成右弓步，同时双拳向上成双贯拳击打甲双耳，目视甲双眼。甲左腿直立，右脚提起绷直放于左膝前上方，同时，双手变掌两臂外格，掌心朝前，力达双臂，目视乙双眼。（如图5-2-11所示）

face, with force directed through to the base of the right palm, and the eyes on B's eyes. B steps into a left bow stance, while switching the left hand to a palm and blocking A's right palm push. Meanwhile, B pulls back the right palm to the waist with the palm facing upward and the eyes on A's eyes. (As shown in Fig. 5-2-9)

Key Points:

A should direct force through to the palm base. B should quickly change step and block A's right palm push with the left palm. The movements should be coordinated and synchronized.

8. B's Kick with Clenched Fist, A's Hook Hand in Falling Step

Movement Description:

B clenches the hands into fists and positions them next to the waist, while lifting the left foot to kick toward A's groin and looking into A's eyes. Then, A turns the body 90 degrees to the right, bends the right knee, and squats into a left flat stance. Simultaneously, A lowers the right palm, moves it from the front of the right knee to the back, and changes it into a hook hand placed behind the waist, with the fingertips pointing upward. A then moves the left arm across the face in coordination with the right arm, with the palm placed in front of the right shoulder, and the eyes on B's eyes. (As shown in Fig. 5-2-10)

Key Points:

A quickly turns into a flat stance to avoid B's kick. B directs force through the heel with focused eyes.

9. B's Double Piercing Punch in Bow Stance, A's Double Open Door by Standing on One Leg

Movement Description:

B steps with the right leg into a right bow stance, while punching fists upward, attacking A's ears, and looking into A's eyes. A stands on the left leg, lifts the right foot straight up in front of the left knee, and changes both hands into palms and performs an outward block with palms facing forward with force directed through to both arms and the eyes on B's eyes. (As shown in Fig. 5-2-11)

Key Points:

A keeps the supporting leg stable, with force directed through to both arms. B exerts force on both arms simultaneously, with force directed through to the fist wheel.

图5-2-11
Fig. 5-2-11

动作要点：

甲支撑腿稳固，力达双臂；乙双臂同时用力，力达拳轮。

10. 甲左弓步英雄坐山，乙左弓步英雄坐山

动作说明：

甲右脚提起向左脚内侧并步震脚，同时左脚离地，双手前臂十字交叉相合击于腹前，接上动不停，左脚向左跨步落成马步并快速变成弓步，同时右拳经胸前向上格挡架于头右外侧，拳心朝下，左拳左下格，停置于左膝上，拳背朝前，拳心朝后，目视乙双眼。乙右转180度，同时右脚提起向左脚内侧并步震脚，同时左脚离地，双手前臂十字交叉相合击于腹前，接上动不停，左脚向左跨步落成马步并快速变成弓步，同时右拳经胸前向上格挡架于头右外侧，拳心朝下，左拳左下格，停置于左膝上，拳背朝前，拳心朝后，目视甲双眼。（如图5-2-12所示）

动作要点：

甲乙震脚有力、动作协调连贯，眼睛有神。

10.A's Hero Sitting on Mountain in Left Bow Stance, B's Hero Sitting on Mountain in Left Bow Stance

Movement Description:

A lifts the right foot, brings it alongside the inside of the left foot, and stomps firmly while lifting the left foot off the ground and crossing both forearms in front of the abdomen. Without any pause, A steps to the left with the left foot, landing in a horse stance and quickly transitioning into a bow stance. Simultaneously, A moves the right fist upward across the chest and stops above the right side of the head to block, with the fist heart facing downward. A also moves the left fist downward to the left, and rests it on the left knee with the fist back facing forward, the fist heart facing backward, the eyes on B's eyes. B turns 180 degrees to the right, brings the right foot toward the inside of the left foot, and stomps firmly while lifting the left foot off the ground and crossing both forearms in front of the abdomen. Following the previous movement, B steps to the left with the left foot, landing in a horse stance and quickly transitioning into a bow stance. Simultaneously, B moves the right fist upward across the chest and stops above the right side of the head to block, with the fist heart facing downward. B also moves the left fist downward to the left, and rests it on the left knee with the fist back facing forward, the fist heart facing backward, the eyes on A's eyes. (As shown in Fig. 5-2-12)

Key Points :

Both A and B stomp their feet forcefully. Their movements are coordinated and continuous, with focused eyes.

图5-2-12

Fig. 5-2-12

11. 甲、乙收势

动作说明：

甲右转90度，左脚收回与右脚并步而立，同时两拳变掌以左手背相击右掌心于头顶上方，向两侧分掌下落，双掌变拳，收于腰间，目视前方。乙左转90度，右脚收回与左脚并步而立。同时，两拳变掌以左手背相击右掌心于头顶上方，向两侧分掌下落，双掌变拳，收于腰间，目视前方。（如图5-2-13所示）

11.A and B Concluding Form

Movement Description:

A turns 90 degrees to the right and brings the left foot back to the right foot. At the same time, A opens both fists into palms, strikes the back of the left hand against the right palm above the head, then lowers the palms while transforming them into fists, placing them next to the waist, and gazing forward. B turns 90 degrees to the left and brings the right foot back next to the left foot. Simultaneously, B opens both fists into palms, strikes the back of the left hand against the right palm above the head, then lowers the palms to the sides while transforming them into fists, placing them next to the waist, and gazing forward. (As shown in Fig. 5-2-13)

图5-2-13

Fig. 5-2-13

后　记

《中华源·河南故事》中外文系列丛书《少林拳法入门》分卷是由中共河南省委外事工作委员会办公室委托河南省中华武术文化外译与传播研究院共建单位——嵩山少林武术职业学院在职教师编写的一本可供海内外武术爱好者学习少林拳的入门教程。本书共分为五个章节。第一章为少林拳概述，主要介绍少林拳的历史发展、技法特点和练拳旨要。第二章为少林拳基础技术技法，其中包括习练少林拳的基本手型、步型及基本技法。这些动作是学习少林武术套路的基础，所谓“练武不练功，到老一场空”。第三章为少林拳基础练习。该部分主要介绍学习少林拳过程中需要重点掌握的组合动作及基本功法。第四章为经典少林拳套路教学。该部分选取了少林拳中比较有代表性的套路，每个套路都由十几个或几十个单势动作组成，动作起伏富有变化。套路编排按照由易到难的顺序。第五章为少林拳实战技法，介绍少林拳在实战中的应用及其攻防含义。

本书采用中英文对照，图文结合的形式编写。武术套路中的每个动作都有详细的动作详解和习练要点。动作详解用文字讲解每个动作的详细过程，说明练习该动作时的身形、手形状态及变化。习练要点则说明在练习该动作时需要重点关注的内容。学习者在使用该教材过程中可图文结合，加深对技术动作的理解。

本书的编写者均有中国境内和海外孔子学院武术教学的经历。编写者在本书的编写过程中，既保持了少林拳传统套路的精髓又兼顾到教学实际，武术套路演示和动作描述尽量做到易学易懂。本书的核心是少林拳中的经典套路罗汉十八手、连环拳及其实战技法，而对理论部分的讲解相对较少，学习者如果需要了解更多关于少林武术的理论知识，可参考《中华源·河南故事·少林功夫》学习。由于经验不足，编写中肯定还存在许多问题，后期使用过程中我们将不断修改完善，力求完美。

随着中外文化交流的深入，越来越多的外国友人开始喜欢并学习少林功夫。米沙拉是坦桑尼亚的一位武术爱好者，2014年在坦桑尼亚达累斯萨拉姆大学孔子学院师从嵩山少林武术职业学院冯俊杰老师学习武术，通过习练少林拳，他真正感受到中国武术的“精、气、神”，感慨“中国功夫太棒了”！通过学习少林功夫让他对中国文化充满了期待。在少林塔沟武术学校的国际教学中心，15岁的越南人美林、22岁的德国人大卫、梦想成为一名“女侠”的法国人小敏与来自印度尼西亚的杨芬妮组成了独特的少林功夫训练队，他们每天早起训练，学习武术套路和少林十八般兵器，业余时间学习中国文化课。充实而又忙碌的学习生活使他们慢慢地爱上了少林武术，他们纷纷表示学成归国后要在当地建立武术俱乐部，带动更多的人来中国学习少林功夫。

少林功夫逐渐在海外“落地开花”，谨以此书献给海内外热爱武术、热爱少林拳法的读者。让我们以武会友，共享中华优秀传统文化。

Epilogue

An Introduction to Shaolin Quan, one volume of the bilingual series of *Chinese Civilization: Stories from Henan* published by the Office of Foreign Affairs Commission of Henan Provincial Committee of the CPC, was compiled by the teaching staff of the Songshan Shaolin Wushu College. This institution is a collaborative entity established with the Henan Institute for Translation and Communication of Chinese Martial Arts Culture. This manual serves as an introductory guide for domestic and international martial arts enthusiasts interested in learning Shaolin quan. The tutorial is divided into five chapters:Chapter One is an overview of Shaolin quan, it primarily discusses the historical development, technical features, and essential principles of practicing Shaolin quan. Chapter Two is basic techniques and skills of Shaolin quan, it includes the basic hand forms, stances, and fundamental techniques of Shaolin quan. These movements form the foundation for learning the routines of Shaolin martial arts, adhering to the principle that "without practicing the foundational skills, a lifetime of martial arts will amount to nothing". Chapter Three is basic practice of Shaolin quan, it focuses on the combination movements and basic skills that are crucial to master in the learning process of Shaolin quan.Chpater Four focuses on classic Shaolin quan routines. It selects some of the most representative ones, each consisting of dozens of individual movements that are rich in variation. The arrangement of the routines follows a sequence from easy to difficult. Chapter Five is Shaolin quan in actual combat. This final chapter introduces the application of Shaolin quan in real combat situations and explains the offensive and defensive meanings behind the techniques.

This book is compiled in a bilingual format, combining both Chinese and English, and integrates illustrations with text. Each movement in the martial arts routines is accompanied by a detailed explanation and key points for practice. The detailed explanation describes the intricate process of each movement in text, explaining the posture, hand shapes, and their transformations during the practice of the movement. The key points highlight the aspects that require special attention while practicing the movement. Learners can deepen their understanding of the technical movements by integrating the text with the illustrations throughout their use of this book.

The authors of this book all have experience teaching martial arts both within China and at Confucius Institutes overseas. During the compilation process, the authors ensured that the essence of traditional Shaolin quan routines was preserved while also considering the practicalities of teaching. The demonstrations of martial arts routines and the descriptions of movements are designed to be as easy to learn and understand as possible. The core of this book focuses on the classic Shaolin routines such as "the Arhat Eighteen Hands", "the Interlinked Fist", and their practical combat techniques, while relatively little attention is given to theoretical explanations. For learners who wish to explore more about the theoretical knowledge of Shaolin martial arts, they can refer to the *Shaolin Kongfu from Chinese Civilization: Stories from Henan*. Due to the lack of experience, there are undoubtedly many issues in the current compilation. We will continue to revise and improve the content during future use, striving for perfection.

As cultural exchanges between China and the world deepen, more and more foreign friends have begun to appreciate and learn Shaolin kungfu. Mishala, a martial arts enthusiast from Tanzania, studied under Master Feng Junjie from Songshan Shaolin Martial Arts Vocational College at the Confucius Institute at the University of Dar es Salaam in 2014. Through practicing Shaolin quan, he truly experienced the essence, energy, and spirit of Chinese martial arts, exclaiming, "Chinese kungfu is amazing!" Learning Shaolin kungfu has filled him with great expectations for Chinese culture. At the International Teaching Center of the Tagou Shaolin Martial Arts School, a unique Shaolin kungfu training team was formed by 15-year-old Meilin from Vietnam, 22-year-old David from Germany, Xiaomin from France, who dreams of becoming a "female knight", and Yang Fenni from Indonesia. They train early every morning, practicing martial arts routines and the eighteen types of Shaolin weapons, while also taking Chinese culture classes in their spare time. Their busy and fulfilling study life has made them fall in love with Shaolin martial arts. They all expressed their desire to establish martial arts clubs in their home countries after completing their studies and to encourage more people to come to China to learn Shaolin kungfu.

As Shaolin kungfu gradually takes root and flourishes overseas, we dedicate this book to readers both at home and abroad who love martial arts and Shaolin quan. Let us connect through martial arts and share the outstanding traditional culture of China.

附录：中国历史年代简表

Appendix: A Brief Chronology of Chinese History

中国历史年代简表
A Brief Chronology of Chinese History

<table>
<tr><td colspan="2" rowspan="5">五帝时代
Period of the Five Legendary Rulers
c. 2600 BC-c. 2070 BC</td><td>黄帝 Huangdi (Yellow Emperor)</td></tr>
<tr><td>颛顼 Zhuanxu</td></tr>
<tr><td>帝喾 Diku (Emperor Ku)</td></tr>
<tr><td>尧 Yao</td></tr>
<tr><td>舜 Shun</td></tr>
<tr><td colspan="2">夏 Xia Dynasty</td><td>c. 2070 BC-c. 1600 BC</td></tr>
<tr><td colspan="2">商 Shang Dynasty</td><td>c. 1600 BC-c. 1046 BC</td></tr>
<tr><td colspan="2">西周 Western Zhou Dynasty</td><td>c. 1046 BC-c. 771 BC</td></tr>
<tr><td rowspan="2">东周
Eastern Zhou
Dynasty
770 BC-256 BC</td><td>春秋
Spring and
Autumn Period</td><td>770 BC-476 BC</td></tr>
<tr><td>战国
Warring States
Period</td><td>475 BC-221 BC</td></tr>
<tr><td colspan="2">秦 Qin Dynasty</td><td>221 BC-206 BC</td></tr>
<tr><td rowspan="2">汉
Han Dynasty
206 BC-220 AD</td><td>西汉 Western Han</td><td>206 BC-25 AD</td></tr>
<tr><td>东汉 Eastern Han</td><td>25 AD-220 AD</td></tr>
<tr><td rowspan="3">三国
Three Kingdoms
220 AD-280 AD</td><td>魏 Wei</td><td>220 AD-265 AD</td></tr>
<tr><td>蜀汉 Shu Han</td><td>221 AD-263 AD</td></tr>
<tr><td>吴 Wu</td><td>222 AD-280 AD</td></tr>
<tr><td rowspan="2">晋
Jin Dynasty
265 AD-420 AD</td><td>西晋 Western Jin</td><td>265 AD-317 AD</td></tr>
<tr><td>东晋 Eastern Jin</td><td>317 AD-420 AD</td></tr>
</table>

续表 Continued Table

南北朝 Southern and Northern Dynasties 420 AD-589 AD	南朝 Southern Dynasties	宋 Song	420 AD-479 AD
		齐 Qi	479 AD-502 AD
		梁 Liang	502 AD-557 AD
		陈 Chen	557 AD-589 AD
	北朝 Northern Dynasties	北魏 Northern Wei	386 AD-534 AD
		东魏 Eastern Wei	534 AD-550 AD
		北齐 Northern Qi	550 AD-577 AD
		西魏 Western Wei	535 AD-556 AD
		北周 Northern Zhou	557 AD-581 AD
隋 Sui Dynasty		581 AD-618 AD	
唐 Tang Dynasty		618 AD-907 AD	
五代十国 Five Dynasties and Ten States	五代 Five Dynasties 907 AD-960 AD	后梁 Later Liang	907 AD-923 AD
		后唐 Later Tang	923 AD-936 AD
		后晋 Later Jin	936 AD-947 AD
		后汉 Later Han	947 AD-950 AD
		后周 Later Zhou	951 AD-960 AD
	十国 Ten States 902 AD-979 AD	北汉 Northern Han	951 AD-979 AD
		吴 Wu	902 AD-937 AD
		吴越 Wuyue	907 AD-978 AD
		闽 Min	909 AD-945 AD
		南汉 Southern Han	917 AD-971 AD
		荆南(又称“南平”) Jingnan (Nanping)	924 AD-963 AD
		楚 Chu	927 AD-951 AD
		南唐 Southern Tang	937 AD-975 AD
		前蜀 Former Shu	907 AD-925 AD
		后蜀 Later Shu	934 AD-965 AD

续表 Continued Table

宋 Song Dynasty 960 AD-1279 AD	北宋 Northern Song	960 AD-1127 AD
	南宋 Southern Song	1127 AD-1279 AD
辽 Liao (契丹 Qidan/Khitan)	907 AD-1125 AD	
西夏 Xixia (Tangut)	1038 AD-1227 AD	
金 Jin	1115 AD-1234 AD	
元 Yuan Dynasty	1206 AD-1368 AD	
明 Ming Dynasty	1368 AD-1644 AD	
清 Qing Dynasty	1616 AD-1911 AD	
中华民国 Republic of China	1912 AD-1949 AD	
中华人民共和国 People's Republic of China	1949 AD-	